Social Problems in

Fred K. Fleagle

Alpha Editions

This edition published in 2023

ISBN : 9789357963039

Design and Setting By
Alpha Editions
www.alphaedis.com
Email - info@alphaedis.com

Contents

FOREWORD

IT would seem presumptuous, even after ten years of residence in Porto Rico, to attempt to classify the social problems of the Island and offer suggestions as to their solution, were it not for the fact that this work does not claim to be a complete and final analysis of the situation, but is designed merely to gather up the material available, and present it in such form that it may be made the basis of class-room study. The absence of such a collection of data was a handicap to the author in his work in rural sociology in the University of Porto Rico, and this book represents, in a somewhat abbreviated form, the material covered. The fundamental principles of sociology are touched on but lightly, since there are already available many excellent books presenting this phase of the subject. It is expected that the instructor will supplement by references and discussions, using the facts presented here to bring out the general principles of theoretical sociology.

It is to be understood that the facts and data presented here are not to be taken as a criticism of Porto Rico or of the Porto Ricans. They are merely an exposition of the social situation as it exists, and do not differ greatly, either in quantity or character, from similar facts which could be gathered relating to any country. It is necessary, however, to know our troubles if they are to be corrected, and we deceive no one if we claim a state of human perfection which does not exist. Neither do we relieve ourselves of responsibility for our own mistakes by calling attention to the fact that other people have made greater ones than we have. A frank facing of the situation, the acknowledgment of whatever there may be that is unpleasant in a social situation, and a sincere desire and attempt to make corrections, is the only honest thing to do.

I have always been optimistic for the future of Porto Rico. It is an island endowed by Nature with more than the usual amount of beauty and brightness. My relations with the people of Porto Rico have been such as to convince me that they have absorbed much of the natural atmosphere of brightness and sunshine which is their heritage, and I believe them sons and daughters worthy of such a beautiful and pleasant island home as Porto Rico.

It will be noted that the emphasis in the following pages has been placed on rural problems. This does not mean that there are more social problems in the country than in the towns, but so little has been done regarding country problems, and the course for which this material was used as a basis being devoted to rural social problems, no attempt was made to take up a discussion of the many topics which might be found in the urban situations.

Special acknowledgment is made for the material used from the reports of Drs. Ashford and Gutierrez, and for the data from the reports of the Insular Bureau of Labor while under the direction of Mr. J. Clark Bills, Jr. Some of this material is quoted verbatim from the reports, and the author does not wish to claim it as his own.

FRED K. FLEAGLE,

University of Porto Rico

POPULATION

THE Island of Porto Rico, covering an area of about 3,500 square miles, had in 1910 a total population of 1,118,012. The population was divided between the towns and country as follows: Urban population 224,620, or 20.1 per cent of the total number, and rural population 893,392, or 79.9 per cent of the total number. From these figures it is evident that the greatest problems of Porto Rico—those which affect nearly 80 per cent of the population—are problems connected with rural life. Of course, many of the people classified as rural inhabitants do not fall strictly within this class, as by urban centers we mean towns with a population of 2,500 inhabitants or more, and thus many of the smaller towns, which really have the advantages of town life, are classified officially as rural centers.

The population of Porto Rico is 65.5 per cent, or nearly two thirds, white, 30 per cent mulatto, and 4.5 per cent black. It is 98.9 per cent native and 1.1 per cent foreign born. During the period from 1899 to 1910 there was an increase in the total population of the Island of 17.3 per cent, which covered an increase of 25 per cent for the native whites, a decrease of 14.5 per cent for the foreign born whites, a decrease of 15.4 per cent for the blacks, and an increase of 10.1 per cent for the mulattoes. The decrease in the number of foreign born whites is due to the fact that in the census of 1899 this group included persons born in the United States, while in 1910 these were classified as natives. The decrease in the number of blacks is doubtless due to intermarriage with other classes, and as a result we have the children of such marriages classified as mulattoes. If the number of such marriages were sufficiently great, the births of blacks would be insufficient to offset the deaths, and the number of blacks would, in that case, necessarily decrease. On this assumption we might very well prophesy that within a few generations the black population in Porto Rico will absolutely disappear, and that we shall have an increased number of mulattoes who, in their turn, will tend to disappear, as they mingle in marriage with people of less colored blood, and in time the black race will be practically absorbed by the whites.

Of the foreign countries represented, Spain, with 56.3 per cent of the total foreign born, leads the list. Cuba and the other West Indies have 20.5 per cent to their credit, France 5.8 per cent, Italy 3.1 per cent, England 2.9 per cent, Germany 1.9 per cent, Denmark 1.6 per cent, while no other single country contributes so much as one per cent to the foreign born population.

The total number of foreign born in 1910 was 11,766. The rural population of 893,392 was divided among the races as follows: Whites 604,541, blacks 32,918, mulattoes 255,923. Thus we see that the great majority of the rural population is of the white race, due no doubt, to the fact that the colder climate of the highlands of the interior does not agree with the hereditary love which the colored race has for a warm climate.

The population of Porto Rico comprises a mixture of bloods and races that complicates the social problems of the Island. The French, Italian, and Spanish elements have tended to mix with the descendants of the Indians originally found here, and to this has been added in many cases a mixture of the blood of the colored race, introduced as slaves into the Island. In some cases the races from the north of Europe have also mingled, so that to-day it is inaccurate to speak of the Porto Ricans as a people of one blood, and the characteristics of the people might be called a composite of the various race elements which have entered into the formation of the native population.

The geographical and geological formation of the Island renders it chiefly agricultural. Little is found in the way of mineral deposits, and manufacturing on a large scale will never be carried on, due to the lack of fuel supply and water power. The climate is agreeable and has no doubt tended to render the people less active than would have been the case in a colder climate. The prevalence of anemia and malaria throughout the Island has also weakened the productive ability of the people and has caused the casual observer to classify the Porto Rican countryman as unambitious and lazy. The loss of vitality caused by the diseases just mentioned, together with others which have visited the Island from time to time, is almost impossible to determine, but there is no doubt but that the laziness with which the Porto Rican countryman is credited, disappears with great rapidity when his system has been freed from the effects of disease.

The Island imports a great part of its food supply, although food stuffs of a vegetable nature are easily produced and might be raised in sufficient quantity to maintain our present population. The Island is too small to provide grazing areas for large numbers of cattle.

The problems of the rural population have been practically untouched up to the present time, as the dominating element in the social and political life of Porto Rico has come from the towns. The rural people have consequently lacked stimulus for self-improvement, inasmuch as there was nothing done to make them dissatisfied with their condition and lead them to try to better it. A system of rural schools has been established by the Department of Education, but not in sufficient number to accommodate all of the children of the country. The solution of the rural situation depends upon proper schooling, a system of instruction which will fit the children for living better rural lives and which shall not be simply the graded system of the towns transplanted to the country. The special problems of the country should be taken into consideration in working out the course of study for the schools, and specially trained teachers should be provided,— teachers who will look upon their work in the rural school as their profession in life, and who will make every effort to adapt themselves to the needs of the community in which they may be located. A continuation of the work which the Government has already started to improve the sanitary and hygienic conditions under which the country people live, the abolishing of anemia and malaria through continuous effort, and instruction as to proper diet and care of the body, together with instruction as to how to secure the necessary kinds of food seems to be the only solution to the rural situation. Certain other problems which relate to the rural family will solve themselves as the educational and economic situation is bettered.

THE JÍBARO

THE rural population of Porto Rico may be roughly divided into the landowners, or planters, and the wage-earning countrymen. The planters are usually people who in many ways closely resemble the country gentleman or squire of England. They are people of considerable importance in their communities, frequently well educated and widely traveled, men who do not hesitate to spend their money freely for their comfort and that of their families when the crops are plentiful and the prices good. They exercise a sort of patronage over the country people who work for them, many of whom live in houses on land provided by the landlord. The laborers look to the landlord for guidance and for advice in practically all matters pertaining to their economic life, and the planter usually reciprocates by caring for the welfare of the countryman to the best of his ability.

Many of the planters, especially such as are located in the coffee districts, have been badly handicapped by the partial destruction of their coffee plantations through cyclones, and by the low price for their product, since they have had to compete with South American coffee in the European and American markets. In addition to this economic disadvantage, the planters are also handicapped by the infirmity of their laborers, most of whom are sufferers from anemia, and few of whom are able to work without the immediate direction of a foreman. The economic and social condition of the planters is not a matter of particular interest to us in this connection, inasmuch as they are so situated that they enjoy all of the advantages of an advanced stage of civilization. The problem that confronts the progress of Porto Rico is to be found in the day laborer of the country districts. The following is taken from the book on *Uncinariasis in Porto Rico*, by Doctors Ashford and Gutierrez:

"Our patient has been in times past the *jíbaro* and will be in time to come. As we have seen already, while all country districts furnish an incredible number of sick, the great breeding places of *necator americanus* are the coffee plantations, and this is the home of *el palido* (the pale man) of Porto Rico.

"The *jíbaro* is a type to be well studied before we essay to interest him in bettering his own condition. Many have written of his virtues, many of his defects, but few, even in Porto Rico, have seen through the mist of a pandemic the real man beyond.

"Coll y Toste says that the origin of the word *jíbaro* proceeds from a port in Cuba (Jibara), and that it is composed of two words of Indian origin, *jíba*, meaning mountain, and *ero*, man. We cannot see the necessity of invoking this port of Cuba with the excellently applicable philology he gives us.

"Brau says that the term is applied to-day to a laborer, but that its true significance is 'a mountain dweller.'

"Our understanding of the term, as it is applied to-day, is a peasant, a tiller of the soil, a man whose life is not that of the town, and who lacks its culture. And when we say that a man is a *jíbaro*, we put him in a separate and distinct class, a class of country laborers. These people 'live now as they lived 100 or 200 years ago, close to the soil.' The *jíbaro* is a squatter and does not own the land upon which he builds his modest house, nor does that house cost him anything save the trouble of building it. It is a framework of poles, with walls of the bark of the royal palm (the *yagua*), with roof of the same material or of a tough grass which is used for thatching, and with a floor of palm boards. Generally the floor is well raised from the ground on posts, and the family is truly a poor and miserable one which is content to have an earthen floor. As a rule, there is but one room for a family, which rarely goes below five, and whose upper limit is measured by the accommodation afforded for sleeping. The cooking is done under a shed on a pile of stones. Weyl says that the house should be valued at about $20.

"The food of the *jíbaro* is poor in fats and the proteids are of difficult assimilation, being of vegetable origin, as a rule.

"He arises at dawn and takes a cocoanut dipperful of *café puya* (coffee without sugar). Naturally, he never uses milk. With this black coffee he works till about twelve o'clock, when his wife brings him his breakfast, corresponding to our lunch. This is composed of boiled salt codfish, with oil, and has one of the following vegetables of the island to furnish the carbohydrate element: banana, platano, ñame, batata or yautia.

"At three in the afternoon he takes another dipperful of coffee, as he began the day. At dusk he returns to his house and has one single dish, a sort of stew, made of the current vegetables of the island, with rice and codfish. At rare intervals he treats himself to pork, of which he is inordinately fond, and on still rarer occasions he visits the town and eats quantities of bread, without butter, of course.

"Of all this list of country food there are only three elements that are bought—rice, codfish, and condiments. Rice is imported from the United States and codfish from Nova Scotia. The bread he eats on his visits to town is made of American flour.

"This is a normal *jíbaro* diet. With the wage paid him he can get no better, but aside from this he is wedded to cheap bulky foods, chiefly for reasons to be stated, and is completely ignorant of the importance of certain foods which any hygienist would like to add to his bill of fare. If the normal food of the *jíbaro*, as stated, were his usual food, it would not be so serious a matter, nor would the *jíbaro* complain so bitterly of his wretched ration, but the fact is he does not get the menu detailed above save when he can be said to be prosperous. Only a few cents difference in wages will cut out the small proportion of animal proteids he obtains, the codfish, and a cyclone will drive him in sheer desperation to the town.

"Aside from all this, if wages were better, it is said, he would leave his ration as it now is and spend his surplus otherwise. This has not been given, however, a very earnest trial. He takes also more rum than he is given credit for by those who have accepted the formula that the *jíbaro* does not drink, but it is true that he is not usually intemperate in this sense. One of his vices is *la mascaura* (the wad of tobacco), and he believes the juice of the tobacco to be beneficial in warding off tetanus.

"The *jíbaro*, mountain bred, avoids the town whenever possible, avoids the genteel life of a civilization higher than that of his own. He instinctively tucks his little hut away in the most inaccessible spots; he shrinks from the stranger and lapses into stolid silence when brought face to face with things that are foreign to his life. He does this because he has been made to feel that he must do all that he is told to do by established authority, and he knows that this authority never takes the trouble to look for him unless it expects to get something out of him; because he is suspicious of outsiders, having been too often led astray by false prophets and disappointed by broken promises; because he realizes that he is not a free agent anywhere save in the mountain fastnesses. In other words, he seeks liberty in his home, freedom from the constant repression of those he recognizes as his superiors, and exemption from a repetition of deceptions that have been so often practiced upon him. He has always been made to stay strictly in his class, in the *jíbaro* class. Frequently when he tries to express himself he is laughed down, frowned down, or growled down. '*Tu eres un jíbaro*' is not a term of reproach exactly, but it means 'You are not in a position to express yourself, for you are only a mountaineer. You know nothing of our world; you are still a child. Your place is under the shade of the coffee tree; the mark you bear is clear to everyone; you are a *jíbaro*.' Thus there is a great difference between the *jíbaro* and those who are not *jíbaros*, i.e., those who live in towns or those who command in the country. This distinction is neither made unkindly nor roughly. All the Porto Rican people are kindly and they love their *jíbaros*, but nevertheless they treat them as though they were children. And the *jíbaro* loyally follows his educated, emancipated fellow citizen, perfectly satisfied to be guided as the latter sees fit.

"Much of this guidance is excellent, and it is not our mission to seek to break down barriers which to-day, may be needful. The *jíbaro* is respectful and obedient, fearful of the law and never defiant of his superiors; he is generous to a fault, sharing with any wayfarer his last plantain; he is devoted to his family and to his friends. Had he been ill treated by the educated and controlling class in the island he would be sullen and savage, but this has not been the case. If it is true that the *jíbaro* is in many ways differentiated from the upper classes, it is equally true that there is no masonry so strong as that existing among the *jíbaros* of Porto Rico. Bound to each other by the most intricate ties of relationship and by a still more potent one, the eternal bond conferred by the title *compadre* or godfather, they share their troubles and shield each other as though they belonged to one great family. It is really wonderful to see how quickly and with what complete self-abnegation an orphaned child or widowed mother is gathered into some poor neighbor's hut and there cared for. For these very same reasons search for a miscreant in the mountains is a formidable undertaking. On inquiry no one knows him, never saw him, never even heard of him, and the closest scrutiny of their faces will not detect the faintest trace of interest or even of intelligence.

"Care must be taken in deducing facts from questioning a group of *jíbaros* even in the most unimportant matters. They are tremendously suspicious and generally let someone among them who is *leido* (one who has established a local reputation for worldly wisdom) speak for them. One can be pretty sure that the rest will say 'amen' to all of his remarks. It is said that this deep suspicion of a strange investigator proceeds from the methods employed by the Spanish *guardia civil* or rural guard, to run down those suspected of unfaithfulness to the administration, petty infringement of the law, etc.

"The *jíbaro* is equally superstitious and very quickly impressed by a supernatural explanation of any phenomena he cannot understand. The more outlandish the explanation of a disease the better he likes it, and for this reason the *curandero* or local charlatan is so popular and powerful in the mountains. We very much fear that our abrupt tumbling in the dust of an ancient explanation of his for anemia, our assertion that it was due to 'worms' and our administration of 'strong medicine' which practically put him *hors de combat* for the day, accounts for part of our early success. In spite of this lack of knowledge of the world above him he has one quality which is his ever ready defense, his astuteness. There is one phrase much used in describing the *jíbaro's* acuteness of observation. Referring to a trade it is said: '*Para un jíbaro, otro, y para los dos, el demonio,*' which means, 'To get the best of a jíbaro, employ another, and to catch both, Satan himself must take charge of them.'

"This astuteness, despite all of the great obstacles in the path of our work among them, was what chiefly led to success in bringing these people under treatment. They soon saw that we got results, and with a fact capable of sensational proof in our hands, the *jíbaro* accepted us and we joined the 'order' to which we have made reference. From that time he has been our friend, and better friends no man ever had, for his entire support is given us; he preaches our 'new medicine' and wherever we have expounded these things to him by word of mouth and by virtue of proof he takes pride in explaining, better than any representative of the upper classes, how the disease is acquired and how it may be prevented.

"The prime fact, however, is that he has, until recently, been much neglected, neglected by those who are not of his class, neglected by the authorities. There are municipalities whose town forms but a tenth of the population of the outlying country, whose taxes are collected to support it, yet which seem to forget the submerged mass in the mountains. This being so for the towns which are surrounded by these people, how attenuated the interest becomes in the capital and larger cities of the island, and how extremely diluted that of the continental American who neither knows his needs nor even what *jíbaro* means.

"Education will transform this *jíbaro* into something much better or much worse, for he will not remain content as he is when he can read, write, and see the world with his own eyes. In this education the respect he bears his more fortunate compatriots, the power for good they have over him, and the confidence he reposes in them must be preserved. The labor he must perform to enrich the island must be dignified by his employer and by himself, or else the hills will be deserted and the *jíbaro* will become a vicious hanger-on of towns. Better homes, better means of communication with towns, now becoming an accomplished fact, better food, education, in which remarkable progress is being made at this day, better habits of life, especially in the modern prevention of disease, must form a part of any plan adopted to improve his condition. The planter who to-day sees the laborer must see in him the man whose bodily, mental, and moral development will make the plantation a success. The planter is the man of all men in Porto Rico who must begin to help the *jíbaro* upward in order to emerge from his own present industrial depression. This lack of mental contact, of a common ground of interest between the *jíbaro* and the better class of Porto Ricans drives the former to charlatans for his medical advice, to the wild fruits and vegetables of the interior for his food, and to weird creeds for his religious comfort.

"His dependency causes him to look for protection, for direction and for ideas from the planter, from the municipality, and from the Insular Government. He considers himself a ward of his employer and of those placed in authority over him. He does not care to accept any responsibility for the simple reason that he has always been made to feel that he is not a responsible person. Therefore, how can we blame him when we find him without shoes, knowing that by wearing them he will protect himself against a dangerous infirmity; without bacon and corn, without household furniture, with but one room for his entire family.

"It is a specious excuse, nothing more nor less, which avers that the *jíbaro* is born the way he is and cannot be changed at this late day, that we must await a new generation, etc. On that principle we could expect very little from the antituberculosis crusades in New York. The truth is that to change the *jíbaro*, we must convince him that he will be bettered by the change, and he is sharp enough to change then, but the gist of all is that these changes must be begun by the men to whom the *jíbaro* has always looked for light, and this means good hard work and much perseverance, tact, and genuine personal interest. From our acquaintance with the men to whom this burden will fall we should say that they are not only sufficiently good business men to realize the benefit they would get out of a healthy laboring class, but that the innate patriotism of the Porto Rican agriculturist and the deeper underlying sympathy for his *jíbaro* will some day bring about reforms that they alone can make possible.

"Agricultural laborers, in spite of the small wages they receive, are nearly if not quite as expensive as those in the United States, for with 50 per cent less of efficiency from disease and wasteful methods of work, the difference in wage is of small advantage. Weyl states:

'The small equity which the planter holds in the estate which he cultivates does not permit him to pay any higher wages, and the poverty of the planter prevents him from making the outlay necessary for the proper cultivation of his land.'

"Few coffee planters have anywhere near a reasonable amount of their land under cultivation for the reason that with the poor help and methods now existent they are unable to extend their plant. The regular labor, employed all the year round, the peons—who form a relatively small percentage of the entire number available for work—are paid for a full day's work, and their degree of anemia is such as to prevent their doing but about 50 per cent of what they are paid for doing. Our estimate of the relative efficiency of labor was made from what the planter himself told us and by a simple experiment which we tried upon about 500 adult workers in different parts of the interior. We questioned each one as to the amount of coffee he could pick in a day and found that from two to three *almudes* was the utmost the majority could do, and that one *almud* was too much for many. Some stated that after picking a sack full in a remote part of the plantation they were unable to get it in to the mill without a mule, on account of the fact that their limbs refused to bear them up. When these people were working at light work, and at a time when the more they picked, the greater the profit to themselves, is it reasonable to suppose that when working for a wage without this incentive this 50 or 60 per cent labor would be any more efficient? This reduction in laboring capacity demonstrates what a heavy toll is paid by both employer and employee to uncinariasis in Porto Rico.

"As to absentee landlords, Weyl says:

> 'Many of the absentee owners of Porto Rican properties and many of their agents in Porto Rico consider the island and its population as equally fit for the crassest exploitation, and are as contemptuous of the people as they are enthusiastic about the island. The current use by many Americans of an opprobrious epithet for Porto Ricans bespeaks an attitude which takes no account of the human phase of the problem, but considers the population as composed merely of so many laborers willing to work for such and such a price.'

"Thus the poor laborer, his earning capacity cut down by his disease, with employment which is at best very irregular, with his sick wife and children for whom he has to buy 'iron tonics' that cost all that he can rake and scrape together, without money for clothes, much less for shoes, with a palm-bark hut not too well protected against the damp cold of the grove in which he lives, with not a scrap of furniture save, perhaps, a hammock, and, worst of all, with a miserable diet lacking in proteids and fats, lives from day to day, saving nothing, knowing nothing of the world beyond his plantation, working mechanically simply because he is not the drone he has been too frequently painted outside of Porto Rico, but without any object save to keep on living as generations have done before him. It has been our experience that when he is asked 'Why have you sought our dispensary?' the answer has almost invariably been, 'Because I can no longer work.' The *jíbaro*, nevertheless, has ever been the lever which has raised the bank account of Porto Rico, and with an average of 40 per cent of hemoglobin and two and a half millions of red corpuscles per cubic millimeter he has labored from sun to sun in the coffee plantation of the mountains, in the sugar estate of the coast land, and in the tobacco field of the foothills, in addition to his personal coöperation in other industries and commercial enterprises. He is a sick man and deserves our highest respect, and merits our most careful attention as a vital element in the economic life of the island. The American people should take seriously into account his future, which is at present anything but promising."

OVERPOPULATION

WHEN we say that a country is overpopulated we speak in relative terms, inasmuch as the overpopulation of a country does not depend upon the density of the population alone, but also upon the ability of that country to produce a sufficient amount of foodstuffs to maintain its population. Thus a country which has a relatively small population and a still smaller ability to produce foodstuffs would be more overpopulated than a country of similar size with a larger population and a still greater production of foodstuffs.

In considering the case of Porto Rico, we find that the Island contains 8,317 square kilometers of land. The estimated population at the present time is 1,200,000. This gives about 140 persons to the square kilometer as compared with 72 persons in France, 237 persons in Belgium, and 252 in Saxony. If the productive ability of the soil of Porto Rico is as great as that of Belgium and Saxony, we must conclude that Porto Rico is not overpopulated. If for any reason it is less, then the extent of overpopulation increases directly as the soil grows less in productive ability.

Porto Rico has about ten times as many inhabitants per square acre as the average throughout the United States; but the conditions of climate do a great deal to equalize this difference. In the first place, the soil is available in Porto Rico for the production of crops throughout the twelve months of the year, whereas in parts of the United States and in northern Europe the soil is usable for only a portion of the year on account of its unproductive condition during the winter months. Another matter that must be taken into consideration in the question of overpopulation, is the severity of the climate. Where the climate is severe, the country will maintain in comfort a much smaller population than where the climate is as friendly to the human race as we find it in Porto Rico.

Of the population of Porto Rico in 1910, about 75 per cent lived in communities that had less than 500 inhabitants, showing conclusively that the great majority of the people of Porto Rico should be classified as rural inhabitants and that the problems which affect the rural people of Porto Rico are the problems which would affect, to a great extent, the entire Island. Only two cities in the Island have a population of more than 25,000, while only 30 would fall under the head of urban territory, that is, towns which have a population of 2,500 or more.

The rate of increase of population in Porto Rico is far in excess of the rate of increase in the United States, and this is one of the things that must be taken into consideration in considering the question of overpopulation. In the United States the rate of increase among the class of people whose salaries range from $700 to $2,500 is from ten to twelve per thousand. In Porto Rico, the rate of increase is about twenty per thousand.

The following table shows a comparison between the birth rate, death rate, and rate of increase in the United States and Porto Rico, the figures given representing the birth and death rate for every thousand of the population in each country.

United States

	Birth rate	Death rate	Increase
Poor Class:	35 to 40	25 to 35	5 to 10
Intermediate class:	25 to 30	15 to 18	10 to 12
Well-to-do class:	12 to 18	12 to 15	4 to 6

PORTO RICO (1914-15)

Birth rate	Death rate	Increase
39.12	19.72	19 to 20

In order to maintain the population of a country, there must be about 400 children between the ages of one and five years for every thousand women between the ages of fifteen and forty-five. The following table shows how Porto Rico compares in this respect with other countries.

United States 492 children per thousand women

France	409	"	"	"	"
Germany	535	"	"	"	"
England	429	"	"	"	"
Sweden	522	"	"	"	"
Porto Rico	725	"	"	"	"

Thus we see that the rate of increase of the population of Porto Rico is much greater than that of the United States. When we take into consideration the advancement being made in sanitary science in Porto Rico and in the elimination of disease, as well as the increased facilities for caring for sickness, we may expect that the rate of increase here will be augmented each year.

The general opinion is that Porto Rico is so thickly populated that a crisis is inevitable, unless some means is found for remedying the present situation. It does not seem, however, that we are justified in coming to such a conclusion when we consider the much more densely populated countries of Belgium and Saxony. Increased production of the soil due to intensive agriculture, and modern methods of farming, as well as the breaking up of the land into small farms, have been the means of taking care of the vast populations of European countries where climatic conditions are not as favorable as they are in Porto Rico. Of the total acreage of Porto Rico about 94 per cent is in farms, and we find that only 30,000 people are directly dependent upon these farms for their support. Of the total number of acres included in farm land, about 75 per cent is improved and under cultivation, so that there is still about one quarter of the land that can be devoted to agriculture when it has been connected with markets, or by other means rendered available for this purpose. There are in Porto Rico more than 58,000 farms, 46,779 of which are operated by their owners. These, in the great majority of cases, are small farms and are of the kind which bring the greatest amount of benefit to the Island. Some 10,000 farms are operated by tenants, and these farms also are usually small.

The following table shows the number of farms of various sizes in the Island to-day:

Farms under 5 acres	20,650
Farms from 5 to 9 acres	11,309
Farms from 10 to 19 acres	10,045
Farms from 20 to 49 acres	8,872
Farms from 50 to 99 acres	3,728
Farms from 100 to 174 acres	1,726
Farms from 175 to 499 acres	1,502
Farms from 500 to 999 acres	332
Farms of 1000 acres or more	207

Of the owners and tenants of these farms 44,521 are white and 13,850 are colored. About 95 per cent of all the owned farms are free from mortgage. The average size of the farms in Porto Rico is about 35¾ acres.

The experience of European countries has been that large farms, in a densely populated country are detrimental to the community welfare, because the holding of such farms by a few condemns a large percentage of the population to a dependent condition. As the number of farms decreases, the number of salaried laborers must increase, and as this floating population increases, there is also a tendency for crime to increase, as the man who has no responsibilities as a proprietor of land often lacks the fundamental stimulus to make him observe the laws of his country. The landowner, having obtained even a small parcel of land, has an incentive for hard work, wishing to better his financial condition, while the dependent salaried man, with no visible stimulus for saving, tends to spend his money as fast as it is earned and seldom accumulates any property. To such an extent is the possession of land regarded as a benefit to the individual and an incentive toward good citizenship, that in some European countries the government has made arrangements to loan money to worthy young men for the purchase of small farms on the ground that the government gains a desirable citizen every time that it creates a landholder. The Government of Porto Rico might well take some steps to encourage dependent laborers to accumulate property, either by means of loans to those who desire to purchase property, or by opening up government land for settlement under the Homestead Act.

The rise in the price of land and the fact that the greater part of the land of Porto Rico is devoted to industries which are most productive when conducted on a fairly large scale, has tended to the accumulation of large tracts of land, and legal measures should be enacted against the accumulation of tracts of land of more than 100 or 200 acres, and providing for the distribution of any large tracts in case of the death of the present owner:

At the present time a good deal of the foodstuffs of Porto Rico is imported into the Island while if there were more widely extended division of the land into a large number of small farms, the production of these foodstuffs could be greatly increased, although, of course, this would tend to decrease the production of certain other crops which at present claim the chief attention of the people of Porto Rico.

According to the Report of the Governor of Porto Rico for 1914-15, the division of land among the various industries, as well as the average value per acre of land for each of the industries, is shown by the following table:

Crop	Acreage	Average value per acre
Cane	211,110	$106.95
Coffee	165,170	61.60
Tobacco	18,040	80.81
Pineapples	3,761	105.24
Citrus fruits	5,274	121.78
Coconuts	6,088	118.33
Minor fruits	102,274	27.53

From this table we see that certain industries, such as the cultivation of pineapples or citrus fruits, which can be carried on successfully on relatively small farms, bring practically as high a return per acre as does the production of sugar cane, which is essentially a large farm product. This argument would not necessarily do away with the cultivation of sugar cane, but would tend to increase the cultivation of other crops wherever and whenever the soil and climatic conditions would permit.

An increase in the number of owned farms and a consequent decrease in the number of dependent wage earners, together with the increased production of foodstuffs which such a system of land management would necessarily bring as a result, providing the management of the farms was carried on under modern scientific methods, would, to a great extent, relieve the situation of overpopulation which we now face. Porto Rico can support twice the population which she now has with comparative ease, providing some means is found to relieve the economic situation of the greater part of the people and to prevent the accumulation of wealth in the hands of a comparatively small number. It is estimated at the present time that the wealth of Porto Rico is in the hands of less than 15 per cent of the population, and the remaining 85 per cent are dependent for their living upon daily or monthly wages. Such a situation must be changed or else the question of overpopulation will become indeed serious. There is no particular reason to fear that the population will increase to such an extent that we shall be unable to support ourselves on what the Island may produce; but with the increase of population under present conditions, trouble between capital and labor and between workmen and their employers cannot be avoided.

Emigration as a means of relief to the overpopulation of Porto Rico will not solve the question. In the first place, the Porto Rican people are essentially a home-loving people, clinging closely to family ties and not at all disposed to migrate to other countries. A few cases of Porto Rican families who have moved to other countries have shown that in the majority of instances the migration was not successful. In the second place, in order to relieve the situation at all it would be necessary to provide for the emigration of a large number of families. The removal of 100 or 500 families from Porto Rico would not make any appreciable difference in the economic situation that we find to-day. The average family consists of five people, and the removal of 5,000 unskilled laborers from the Island would not tend to relieve the situation.

The only means of meeting the situation of overpopulation is through increasing the food production of the Island by means of division into small farms, intensive cultivation, and modern methods of farming. The school must do its share in the teaching of small-farm and garden farming, and the Government should assume the responsibility for fostering the increase of the number of small farms as well as for assisting in the educational work to improve the methods of cultivation.

THE FAMILY

THE family is the simplest combination of individuals that we find in organized society and is the basis of social group forms. It ranks in importance as a social institution with the church, the state, and the school, coming into existence before any of these three institutions. It existed in a complete form, consisting of father, mother, and children long before there was such an institution as civil or religious marriage. In the history of mankind, the family and marriage grew up together, the importance of the family requiring certain marriage customs by which the members of the family could be held together to protect the interests of the children.

In Porto Rico we find the average family consisting of five people, and according to the census of 1910, in the total population 15 years of age and over, 43.7 per cent of the males and 38 per cent of the females were single; 36.2 per cent of the males of the total population and 35.4 per cent of the females were married, while 16 per cent of the males (or a total of 50,113), and 15.7 per cent of the females (or a total of 51,073), were consensually married, that is, living together by mutual consent, but without the benefit of a civil or ecclesiastical marriage.[1] This proportion is somewhat lower than it was in 1899, as the percentage of consensual marriages in comparison with the population at that time was 16.3 per cent for the males and 15.2 per cent for the females. The difference, however, does not exceed one half of one per cent, and there were actually 17,046 more people living together consensually in 1910 than in 1899. The seriousness of the situation may be seen when we consider that of the total population of the Island over 15 years of age, 31.7 per cent, nearly one third, representing 101,186 people, are living together without any form of marriage ceremony.

Many reasons have been given for the prevalence of the consensual marriage in Porto Rico, among which are to be found the necessity of the ecclesiastical marriage with its complicated forms and the relatively costly ceremonies which prevailed before the institution of civil marriage under the American Government. It seems quite probable, however, that this custom is a relic of the consensual marriage form, which was established by the early colonizers of Porto Rico, many of whom came to the Island, leaving their families behind, and entered into consensual marriage relations with the native women of the Island. In this way the custom was established, and there was a lack of public opinion against it which has existed down to the present time, and until, through the influence of the schools, public opinion against this form of union can be roused, very little progress will be made in changing conditions.

There is no doubt but that many of the consensual marriages are considered by the parties concerned just as permanent as those performed by civil or ecclesiastical authorities, and the question of immorality does not enter into their view of the situation. It is a question of mutual consent, and especially in the country districts, the knowledge of the law in regard to these matters is very vague. The greatest harm in cases of marriage of this sort lies in the tendency to prevent the spread of public opinion against the custom and in the ease with which the family relations can be broken at the will of either member of the family, with the resulting unprotected condition of the children which may have been born into the family.

The number of persons of illegitimate birth in the Island of Porto Rico, as given by the census of 1899 and that of 1910, is as follows:

White illegitimates 1899   66,855

White illegitimates 1910   76,695

Colored illegitimates 1899   81,750

Colored illegitimates 1910   78,554

Thus we see that there was an actual increase of nearly 10,000 white illegitimate children from the year 1899 to 1910, or an increase of 14.7 per cent; but during the same time the white population had increased 24.7 per cent, so that there was an actual decrease in the percentage, according to population, of nearly 10 per cent. During the same period the colored population had increased 5.9 per cent, but the number of colored illegitimate children had decreased 3.9 per cent, there being actually a less number of colored illegitimate children in 1910 than in 1899, although the population had increased. It seems very probable that this is due to the fact that the great majority of the colored population in Porto Rico is to be found in the towns, where the school system is more efficient than in the country districts and where customs change more easily, due to wider associations and to more frequent and continued intercourse with people of other points of view.

In the country the custom has remained, with little change, due to the fact that the isolation of the country people and the comparatively small number of children in the rural schools has given little opportunity to work against the existing situation. Of the children from the ages of one to ten years there was only an increase of 1,397 white illegitimate children between 1899 and 1910, which was not anywhere near the rate of increase of the white population as a whole. During the same period there was an actual decrease in the number of colored illegitimate children between the ages of one and ten years, amounting to 7,717, or a total decrease of illegitimate children under 10 years of age of 6,320, which would lead us to believe that within the last ten years the births of consensual marriage and the number of illegitimate children have decreased much more rapidly than the total census figures would indicate.

In addition to the question of consensual marriages, we find that under the Spanish administration, when ecclesiastical marriage was the only form recognized, there were no divorces registered in the Island of Porto Rico. With the introduction of the civil marriage after the American occupation, and the institution of divorce laws and the recognition of divorce by the civil authorities, the question of divorce began to demand attention, and in 1910 we find a total of 1,246 divorces among the people in the Island of Porto Rico. About two thirds of these were women,[2] and the divorce question will undoubtedly in time bring as many problems in Porto Rico as it has in the United States.

According to the last report of the Insular Chief of Police, it is estimated that there are in the Island of Porto Rico at the present time about 10,000 homeless children under 12 years of age who live by whatever means they are able, many of them begging or stealing, and most of them having no permanent lodging place, sleeping at night in boxes or on doorsteps, or wherever they happen to find a lodging place secure from the rain. These children are, for the most part, deserted and abandoned children of illegitimate parentage, or orphan children whose parents have left no provision for their care and education, and they constitute a fertile soil for the implanting of criminal tendencies and are ready material for older people of criminal habits. They constitute a danger to the security of the community, and if it were not for the relatively high death rate that is found among people of this class, the Island would soon be overrun by citizens brought up under these criminal-forming conditions. The Insular Government should take measures to reduce this danger by means of the compulsory industrial education of this class of boys and girls. There is enough Government land available to colonize them in different parts of the Island under the care of people trained in reformatory and industrial methods, and this should be done in order that they may become self-supporting individuals who will contribute to the comfort of the community, rather than parasites who live on the charity of others. There are any number of small industries in which they might be trained, as well as along agricultural lines, and the trades which lack skilled workmen in Porto Rico would be much benefited by adding to their number graduates of industrial trade schools, taken from children of this class; these schools should be operated by the Government, at Government expense, but could be made largely self-supporting by means of the sale of the services of the boys, or through the sale of the products turned out.

The living accommodations of the average rural family are very unsatisfactory, consisting, as they do, of a dwelling house of one room, or at the most, two. This reduced house space makes it necessary to eat and live and sleep in the same room, rendering impossible any degree of privacy on the part of any of the family. This condition in the case of growing boys and girls is very undesirable, particularly since it is a custom to take in as members of the family relatives, sometimes of a rather remote degree of relationship, in case they are left unprotected. Another feature of family life which tends toward degeneration and which is found to a great extent in Porto Rico, is the intermarriage between relatives within comparatively close degrees of consanguinity. The civil laws of Porto Rico prohibit the marriage of persons of closer degrees of relationship than first cousins, and the ecclesiastical laws of the Roman Church prohibit marriage within eight degrees of consanguinity. In the record of one family which produced 25 cases of insanity in two generations, it was found that there had been a considerable amount of intermarriage between relatives, one of the grandparents marrying a person who was prohibited by the ecclesiastical law on four different grounds on account of consanguinity. Ecclesiastical permission had been obtained to overcome these difficulties and the marriage took place. There is no doubt that close intermarriage and the failure to introduce new stock into the family tends to both mental and physical degeneration. And where families intermarry for generations, as we find to be the custom in a great many instances in Porto Rico, there can be no doubt of the ultimate disastrous outcome from this custom.

The average Porto Rican family lives very happily and contentedly, the parents displaying great affection for the children and for relatives even of a remote degree of relationship. In the case of the death of parents, relatives usually adopt or take charge of the children which may be left and bring them up as carefully as they would children of their own. The family group is naturally closer among Latin peoples than among Anglo-Saxon races, and this has tended to do away with some of the vices of family life which are found among Anglo-Saxon peoples, while the same circumstances have tended to increase other unsatisfactory conditions of family life peculiar to Latin races.

One of the features which, from the standpoint of society, may have an unfortunate result is the mixture of races in the family life. While this has not taken place to such an extent in the country districts as it has in the towns, nevertheless, a great many families in Porto Rico are composed of mixed races. The biological tendency in cases of mixed races, according to most authorities, is a decrease in the number of children in the family as generation succeeds generation, unless there is an addition of new blood to a considerable extent. This may possibly be one of the means which Nature has provided for solving the problem of overpopulation in Porto Rico, but there is the added fact that usually as the succeeding generations become fewer in regard to numbers, they also become less capable mentally and physically. The race question in Porto Rico will undoubtedly come to be one of the problems that has to be solved, and it will be more difficult of solution than the race problem in the United States, where the races are becoming more widely separated every year and where it is very infrequent to find persons of the two races in the same family. In Porto Rico the problem will be intensified because it is not merely a problem between races, but a race problem which involves the family organization in many cases. The government of Brazil has predicted that in a hundred years there will be no black inhabitants in the Brazilian republic, that they will be entirely assimilated by the white race or carried off by disease. The census report for Porto Rico shows a falling off in the black race of about 9,000 in the last ten years, and an increase of about 30,000 in the mixed or mulatto population. Thus the assimilation of the black population is gradually taking place, and whether this will in time lead to a complete assimilation, or whether the mixed race will become weakened through this racial intermarriage to such an extent that it will eventually refuse to propagate, is a question which only time can answer. There is no doubt, however, that this is one of the problems that must be confronted in Porto Rico.

RURAL HOUSING CONDITIONS

THE housing of a people is always a matter of prime importance in their social life and development. There is little progress until the housing conditions are comfortable and hygienic, and the development of the home and the family life depends to a great extent on the conditions under which a people lives. The housing conditions in Porto Rico, especially for the poorer classes, are far from satisfactory. The dwellings of the country people are described as follows, in the Report on the Housing Conditions in Porto Rico, published by the Insular Bureau of Labor in 1914:

"There are five general problems which the laborer or employer in tropical countries, who is anxious to build cheap but proper houses, has to meet. The first is to provide adequate protection against the heat. As in northern countries it is necessary to shut out the cold winds and generate and conserve artificial heat within the house, so in tropical countries it is equally important to let in the breezes and to clear out any artificial heat that may arise.

"The second problem is to provide protection against the frequent tropical rains. This is especially important in tropical countries that have a protracted rainy season, as it is often difficult to shut out the rain without also shutting out the fresh air.

"The third problem is the provision of adequate sanitary facilities. Due to the heat in southern countries and to the humidity that prevails during certain seasons of the year, this problem is more difficult of solution and likewise more important than in countries farther north.

"The fourth problem is that of securing cheap and durable building materials. In a land like Porto Rico where tropical shrubs and the palm are practically the only woods that the laborers are able to obtain, we must not expect the same solid, commodious habitations which are found in northern countries where the pine and hemlock abound.

"The fifth problem, perhaps as important as any of the preceding and certainly as difficult to remedy, arises partly from the generosity of nature herself. People can live in tropical countries in almost any form of habitation. Cold winters have not obliged the poorer classes to be adepts in house construction. Poverty has forced them to live as cheaply as possible. Naturally, the laboring classes engaged in tilling the soil still make their homes in the cheapest forms of huts. This problem has, therefore, three aspects—an over-indulgent climate, poverty, and a lack of opportunity by the poorer classes to learn better methods of house construction.

"In Porto Rico we have, in addition to the problems mentioned above, two special conditions which have influenced the form and quality of our laborers' houses. The first is that the seasonal character of many of our agricultural industries forces the laborers to migrate from one section to another in order to find work and, naturally, they are not inclined to go to the expense and exertion of building substantial homes. The second, and more important, arises from the fact that the greater part of our laborers do not own the land their houses are placed upon and, being subject to ejection at the will of their landlords, they have no incentive to beautify or improve their homes.

"According to the census of 1910, the urban territory of Porto Rico—that is, the places of 2,500 inhabitants or more—contained 224,620 inhabitants, or 20.1 per cent of the total population, while 893,392 inhabitants, or 79.9 per cent, lived in places of less than 2,500 inhabitants, and of these, 837,725 lived in strictly rural territory. Needless to state, the greater part of the rural inhabitants belong to the laboring classes and live in the types of rural homes described in this section.

"We have divided the habitations of rural laborers, according to their construction, into the following types: (1) Single houses of thatch, (2) single houses of wood and zinc, (3) tenements of wood and zinc.

"Most of the thatched huts in the rural sections have been built by the laborers who live in them. The land upon which these houses are built is, however, usually the property of some plantation or landowner. Only in the more inaccessible sections inland do the laborers who have built these thatched houses also own the land they are placed upon. It is the custom among the landowners to allow laborers who work for them to take the necessary materials—grass, sticks, palm-bark, etc.—from the land and build their huts. This is done, of course, with the consent of the landowner, and the huts so built are legally attached to the land and become the property of the landowner. As a matter of fact, the laborers who have built these huts claim them as their property and are allowed to live in them without charge or molestation so long as they work for the landowner when their services are needed. When a laborer who has built a hut leaves it and moves to another's land, the hut is claimed by the landowner and some other laborer is allowed to move into it. There are also some of these huts that have been built by the landowners at their own expense, but the plantation owners and other landowners who have gone into the business of building houses for their workmen usually construct a better type of house. The thatched hut, therefore, while it is legally a plantation house, is not usually so considered, either by the landowner or the laborer.

"If we judge the importance of a type of house from the number of people who live in it, this thatched hut is far more important than any other rural or urban type. The great mass of the rural laborers live in houses of this type and, as has been shown, fully three-fourths of the total laborers of the Island live in rural sections.

"The homes of the wealthy in all parts of the world are constructed to conform to the standards of the age and place in which they are erected, and to the personal desires of the occupants, regard being taken only of the absolutely necessary conditions of environment. The houses of the poor, on the other hand, are the direct product of local environment. The hut of the inland laborer of Porto Rico, the *jíbaro*, is a striking illustration of the effect of environment upon the type of house in which the poor live.

"The problem of obtaining cheap and durable building materials is a very difficult one for the poor laborers of Porto Rico. Hard woods are extremely scarce, and the poor inland laborer cannot afford to buy imported lumber, and, therefore, he has been obliged to utilize the coarse grasses and the products of the palm trees that are accessible at little or no expense except the labor necessary in their preparation. Furthermore, many of these people have not the skill nor the necessary tools to use materials such as stone and clay which they might be able to obtain. Also, the migratory character of many of these inland laborers, and the fact that they do not own the land their houses are built upon, have been fundamental influences in preventing the development of better house types. The principal agricultural industries, *i.e.*, coffee, sugar, and tobacco, have a busy and a dull season, and many of the inland laborers are obliged to migrate from one section to another in order to find work. For this reason hundreds of laborers pass annually from the inland hills where coffee is grown down to the sugar plantations on the coast, and then back again to the hills, the busy seasons of sugar and coffee being at different times of the year. Of course, these laborers cannot move their houses with them about the Island, and they naturally tend to build the cheapest kind of temporary structures. Also very few of them own the land their houses are placed upon. They are mere squatters, or tenants at will, and the land owner may eject them at any time for little or no cause, so that there is no incentive to build substantial structures, and there is no chance of developing that pride in the home which is so essential to the building of good houses.

"The inland laborers who live in these huts have been their own architects and builders, and they model their homes after the old type that has prevailed among the hills for centuries. The framework of these huts is of poles and small sticks cut from shrub trees and nailed or tied together at the corners with native fiber ropes. The roofs are generally thatched with a long, tough grass, and the walls are constructed by binding leaves of the royal palm (*yaguas*) with sticks and fiber. The floor is of boards or slabs and is raised from one to two feet above the ground. In some sections *yaguas* are also used for the roofs, and in the inland there are many huts with walls of slabs from the trunk of the palm trees. These huts are usually divided into two rooms by a flimsy partition of *yaguas*, one room being used as a bedroom and the other as a combined living and dining room. The kitchen is a separate room or shed at the rear, and, probably because of the danger of fire, is usually without floor. The furniture consists of hammocks, boxes for chairs, a rough table, and a few dishes, all made from gourds, except the iron pot used in cooking. The value of such furniture is usually from $4 to $6, and the value of such a house from $10 to $20.

"This hut of the inland laborer with its thatched roof and open construction is, in many respects, a much better house than the casual observer is likely to believe. A well-constructed thatch roof, when it is new, offers sufficient protection against rain and excellent protection from the heat of the tropic sun. New palm bark walls are also adequate to keep out the rains. Furthermore, almost without exception, the floors are raised above the ground, so that the surface waters after a shower run freely under the hut and wash away any refuse that may have accumulated, and then the sunlight and winds quickly dry the remaining dampness. In other words, a new well-built hut of this type is a properly ventilated, cool, and reasonably sanitary habitation, and represents the best effort of the laborers to adapt themselves, in their poverty-stricken condition, to the circumstances of their environment. On the other hand, these huts deteriorate very rapidly. Within six months or a year, a dozen varieties of insects have made their nests in the thatched roof, the palm-leaves have cracked, and the floor sags.

"One who stands on some projecting point high up on a mountain side in the interior of the Island and carefully scans the hillsides about and the valley beneath, will be amazed at the number of small huts of this type that lie within his view. There are hundreds of them. Every knoll is crowned by its hut; every hillside is dotted by them. No two are ever placed together; each family seeks its own free life. It is practically true that one cannot shout in any part of our Island and not be heard by the occupants of one or more of these huts.

"To say that these people are contented and prefer to live as they do, is not true. Customs clinch themselves upon a people so that they appear contented, and these inland laborers have lived under the same conditions for three centuries. Their standards of living are modest, and their desires are few. In this sense they are contented. Yet there is a deep and powerful change coming over them. They are going to the cities in greater number than ever before; their children are attending the little schools in the hills. New ambitions are awakening. When the dull season comes, they cannot find work. There are times when many of them are hungry. They are not contented.

"That the Porto Rican laborer is of cheerful disposition is especially true of the so-called *jíbaro*. He has been obliged to find his joy in simple things. He greets you with a smile; he welcomes you to his house and cheerfully divides his cup of coffee with you; he dances with a show of gayety on a Sunday afternoon. He is ever cheerful, but not happy. There may be some customs and prejudices of minor importance that he is loath to change, but in the main he prefers to live as he does because he is obliged so to live. Those who adhere to the *laissez faire* policy and believe that conditions are good enough as they are, do not know the real heart of these people. They need and deserve and must ultimately receive the opportunity to improve their living and working conditions.

"There are two important causes for the erection of plantation houses: (1) For the employer, the practical advantage of having a resident supply of labor on his land; (2) for the laborer, the necessity of living near his work. Laborers who live in plantation houses are more largely dependent upon the plantation than are laborers who live in their own homes. One of the conditions of occupying a plantation house is that the occupants will work for the plantation whenever their services are required. Laborers living in plantation houses, can, therefore, be depended upon by their employers, and this is a great advantage to the plantation owner. Furthermore, such houses are usually much better than the laborers who live in them could afford to build for themselves. Frequently, also, the holdings of the plantation are so extensive that it would not be possible for the laborers, even if they had the money, to buy land upon which to build their houses within walking distance of their work.

"There are great differences between the single houses of wood and zinc erected by the various plantations. The better types have been built by employers who wished to provide healthful and comfortable quarters— increase the efficiency of their laborers as well as to hold their labor supply. Unfortunately, at present, such houses are not being erected by the plantations in all parts of the Island. The majority of these houses have been built with the sole purpose of holding as large a labor supply as possible at the least expense.

"The houses of this type are usually roofed with large strips of zinc, nailed directly upon the rafters. These roofs are low, unceiled and, as a result, the houses are extremely hot. The walls are of imported lumber, sometimes the boards being matched and in other cases clapboarded. The better houses are painted to diminish the depreciation and to awaken the pride of the occupants in their homes. The walls are six or seven feet high. The floors are of boards and raised from one to two feet above the ground. The houses are set upon posts so that there is a clear space under them that can be easily cleaned. On the interior they are divided by half partitions into two or three rooms and are usually provided with separate kitchens, frequently one kitchen serving for from one to four houses. These houses cost from $70 to $150, the average being about $80, according to their size and construction. This description refers to the better houses of this type and, unfortunately, the majority of the single plantation houses are not so well constructed.

"These tenements represent the older type of plantation houses and fortunately very few of them are being built at the present time. Their construction has been prompted by the same reason that has induced employers to build the single type of plantation house—the desire to hold a resident supply of labor on the plantation. They are, however, far inferior to the single houses.

"The better rural tenements are built with zinc roofs, board walls and floors, and are raised from one to two feet above the ground. They are unceiled and have no windows. In the inland many of them have zinc walls. The poorer ones are located on low, swampy land and are built of oil cans, pieces of boxes, and other odds and ends. Some of them have separate kitchens and sanitary facilities, but many have nothing except such temporary and inadequate structures as the occupants have themselves built. The first reason for building tenements of this type has been, of course, to house the greatest number of laborers at the least expense. They are long structures, one or two rooms wide, each room an apartment, and crowded with people. Although these rural tenements are not usually being built at present, there are still hundreds of them in use.

"The worst housing conditions upon the plantations prevail in the buildings, usually tenements of this type, set aside as sleeping quarters for unmarried laborers. This type of labor is transient, coming for a few months during the busy season and then passing on to another section of the Island. Consequently, they are crowded into whatever quarters may be available at the time. The leaky rooms of the old sugar mills, the worst rooms in the tenements, single houses that have been unused for six months and are out of repair and filthy, are usually used for the emergency—an emergency that lasts from three to six months. Six, eight, or ten hammocks are hung up between bare walls in a room 10 feet by 15 feet and are all filled each night. Conditions of ventilation and general sanitation are frightful.

"There is one notable exception. One of the largest centrals of our Island has constructed a large, well-ventilated, and comfortable men's apartment. The floor is of matched boards, solid and clean. The walls are also of matched boards, but there is an open space two feet wide at the top of the walls extending around the building. Overhanging eaves prevent the rain from beating in through this opening. The roof is of heavy paper nailed to a thick wooden ceiling. Frames are arranged in the interior of the building for hanging hammocks, and around the walls are large individual lockers for the use of those sleeping there. Finally, the building is cleaned thoroughly every day.

"No description of the housing conditions of rural laborers would be complete without mention of the gardens cultivated by the occupants of the houses. It is safe to say that nine out of every ten laborers in the rural sections, with the exception of those who live in plantation houses where there is no land that they are permitted to cultivate, have planted some sort of garden. It is also true that these gardens are, in most cases, of very little practical use. Well cultivated and productive gardens belonging to rural laborers are hard to find.

"The average garden consists of two or three plantain or banana trees, a few tubers, and some medicinal plants. Frequently, there are many and beautiful flowers. Whatever vegetables there may be are poorly cared for and do not produce more than a third of a proper yield.

"This subject is of tremendous importance. The soil and climate of Porto Rico are such that it should be able, even with its dense population, to produce most of its food. There are unused plots of ground around practically every hut in the interior of the Island. The decrease in the production of sugar is going to throw many laborers out of work and they will be obliged to raise most of their own food or suffer. Many reasons have been advanced to explain the absence of good small gardens. The laborers themselves say that they do not plant and cultivate gardens because they do not own the land and they are allowed to plant only on condition that they give the greater part of their produce to the landowners. They claim also that it does not pay to break up the ground for one crop and that after they have got plantains, etc., growing they may be obliged to move. It is also true that in most cases they have not money enough to buy the seed or hire the oxen and implements needed for breaking up the ground.

"Also, in some parts of the south coast, it is too dry for profitable gardening. On the other hand, landowners frequently say that the reasons why laborers in the rural sections do not plant gardens are lack of knowledge of gardening methods, lack of realization of the benefits that they could derive from good gardens, and custom. Without discussing the relative merits of these reasons, there are two things that must be faced—such laborers must be educated, so far as possible by example, and they must be offered the opportunity to hold land with some fixity of tenure, either by purchasing it on the installment plan or by obtaining leases from the present landowners."

WOMAN AND CHILD LABOR

FORTUNATELY, the factory system has not been introduced to any great extent into Porto Rico, nor in all probability will woman and child labor in factory employment ever constitute a serious problem. The census of 1910 gives only a total of 1912 woman wage earners in various industries of the Island. This, of course, does not include the woman who works throughout the rural districts, and whose condition constitutes the problem which must be studied and remedied in the Island.

The average unskilled laborer in the country districts of Porto Rico does not earn a sufficient sum to enable him to maintain his family in comfort. As a result, the wife, and frequently the children, must contribute to the support of the family as much as they can. In some parts of the Island, the tasks of the country women are largely limited to their housework and the cultivation of whatever garden products they may raise, because such crops as sugar cane do not call to any great extent for the use of woman labor. In other sections of the Island, however, particularly those parts where coffee growing is the chief industry, the gathering and caring for the coffee crop is left, to a great extent, to the women and children. This, of course, results in a financial saving to the coffee grower, as the wages for woman and child labor are much less than for the services of men. The unhealthful results, however, more than offset the advantages gained by adding the mother's wages to the family income.

The harmful results from woman labor may be classified as direct and indirect. Under the directly harmful results are the weakened physical condition of the mother, the increased susceptibility to diseases which are especially common in the coffee districts, particularly anemia, and such diseases as are the results of exposure. The larva of the hookworm lives and finds a fertile field for action in the damp and shady regions devoted to the production of coffee, and as the majority of the women laborers are not accustomed to wear shoes, they easily permit contact and contagion from this disease.

The strength of children and their ability to withstand disease depends to a great extent upon whether or not they are physically strong at the period of their birth and during the time they are under the direct care of the mother. A mother whose system has been weakened by the debilitating effects of anemia, cannot nourish her child and provide him with the necessary amount of food, and as a result, the child is either anemic, or a victim to malnutrition as a result of introducing solid food into his system before the digestive organs are prepared to take care of such food.

Among the indirectly harmful results of woman labor is the necessary separation of the mothers from the children of the family. The mother on going to work, either leaves her children in the care of a neighbor, or leaves them at home where the older children take care of the younger. This deprives the children of the mother's influence and allows them liberty to associate with children who may be undesirable companions, which would be avoided to a great extent if the mother were present to take care of them. The Juvenile Court records in the United States show that 85 per cent of the delinquent children brought before the court have been led into bad habits through the failure of one or both of the parents to take care of their supervision during play hours. Divorce in the United States has been strongly attacked for the reason that it deprives the child of one of his legal protectors. From the same point of view, woman and child labor, which deprives the child of the care of his mother, must inevitably produce bad results in the growing generation.

The use of child labor in Porto Rico is not particularly preferred except in coffee districts and in certain agricultural sections where boys are used at certain times of the year to help drive the oxen, or to help in planting the crop. As this is outdoor work it does not have the devitalizing effect upon the child's body which factory work would have, and as it does not require concentrated attention, it is relieved from the monotony which would tend to lower the child's mental ability. The evil results which must be guarded against are those arising from overwork and from association with undesirable characters while the child is not under the supervision of his parents. In addition to this, the child who is engaged at work must lose the benefits which he should be receiving from attendance at school. During the last year, the Department of Education has attempted to solve this problem by changing the vacation period, so that the long vacation of three months will fall at the coffee-picking season in such sections of the Island as are devoted to the production of this crop, and where previously there was a great decrease in school attendance at the time when the harvesting of the coffee was in progress. This, undoubtedly, will greatly help to do away with the harmful results which formerly were the consequences of irregular attendance or non-attendance at school on the part of a great many of the children in the coffee-growing districts.

An increase in the number of rural schools so that all of the children of the rural districts can be accommodated, is also necessary before this problem is entirely solved. At the present time, a large number of the children in the country cannot attend school, either because the school in the neighborhood is overcrowded, or because the nearest school is at too great a distance for them to attend with regularity. The removal of these conditions unfortunately depends upon an added appropriation for the maintenance of the Department of Education, and it is doubtful whether the income of the Island will be sufficient to supply the needed increase for years to come. With the gradual improvement of roads, consolidated schools may help to solve the problem, and a half-day enrollment for each group will tend to increase the number of children that can be taken care of. Children who find that they cannot obtain a place in the school will naturally be made use of by their parents for wage-earning purposes whenever possible, but the great majority of parents would not put their children at work if the children were enrolled in school and if irregularity of attendance were to lead to dismissal from the school.

Another thing that would help to relieve the situation, as far as woman and child labor is concerned, would be the establishment of a minimum wage for unskilled farm labor, such wage to be sufficient to enable the laborer to maintain his family without the help of money earned by the wife or children. The time of the wife could be occupied in poultry raising and in caring for the family garden, which would also tend to reduce the cost of living for the family and could easily be established, if the landowner were to provide sufficient garden space with each house in addition to the regular wages paid his laborers. Of course, methods of gardening would have to be included in the rural school programs, and the rural teacher should act as a supervisor of these gardens and advisor to the people of the community in which he is employed.

The important things to guard against in the life of the family, from the standpoint of the welfare of both the family and the community, are that the mother need not be obliged to dissipate the strength, through outside labor, which she needs in the raising and caring for her family. The lack of proper supervision of the children through the absence of the mother from the home must also be guarded against. In case it can be proved that a father is unable through his own efforts to earn sufficient to maintain his family, a system of mothers' pensions carried on by the government should be established in order that the mother may be safeguarded from want in case of the death of her husband, and that she may not be obliged to help him in the maintenance of the family through the performance of such labor as would interfere with her regular family obligations.

INDUSTRIES

THE principal industries of Porto Rico are necessarily of an agricultural character, and their importance to the Island financially is shown by the fact that during the year 1914-15 exports to the value of $49,356,907 left for the United States and foreign countries. The imports for the same period reached the amount of $33,884,296, thus giving a good surplus to the Island after the total imports had been paid for. The principal classes of imports are the foodstuffs which might be produced in sufficient quantities to maintain the population of Porto Rico. This is a situation which should receive attention, inasmuch as the Island is capable of producing all of the foodstuffs which it needs for its own consumption. The principal article of export from Porto Rico is sugar and other products of the sugar cane. The article of export second in value is tobacco in its various forms. Third comes coffee; and these three products make up the chief source of wealth.

The chief criticism in regard to the agricultural situation of Porto Rico at the present time, is that there has been very little development of small farm products which would tend to make it possible and profitable for the landholder who is in possession of only a few acres to earn a comfortable living. The climate and soil of Porto Rico would, undoubtedly, lend themselves to the production of many fruits and vegetables which could be raised with profit on farms limited in size, and which would enable the small farmer to maintain his family.

In addition to the introduction of agricultural products fitted for small farm production, an opportunity should be given and efforts encouraged for the establishment and improvement of such lines of work as can be carried on in the homes or by a small group of people working independently. Among these kinds of work are several, such as the hat-making and basket-making industries, the production of handmade lace and embroidery, and other forms of needlework, which might be carried on by women working independently during the time they have free from the occupations of their household work. These handmade articles of Porto Rico are much sought after by tourists, and there is no doubt but that a large and profitable market could be opened for them in the United States, if efforts were made to establish the production on a commercial basis. The individual living in a small town who devotes himself to hat making is handicapped because he has no steady market for his goods and is obliged to sell them or trade them for whatever he can obtain from retail dealers, who themselves attempt to secure only the limited trade which enters their stores. In order to make industries of this sort profitable to the producers, it will be necessary to secure a new and permanent market for the goods, and either the government or some group of individuals who will not exploit the workers, should act as middlemen to see that the work is uniform in character, and to attend to the handling of the finished products and the supplying of a market for it in the United States. Working as individuals, the countrymen or dwellers in small towns have turned out products which differ in quality and in design, and very frequently the lack of resources has obliged them to construct their products from unsuitable or cheap materials.

They have been accustomed to ask for their products as high a price as they thought they could obtain, and often this price is too high for the quality of the article, while sometimes it does not pay for the labor and time which has been expended in the production of the article. By systematizing the work and putting it under the direction of competent supervisors who would specify the quality of material to be used in the production of the articles, and who would fix a price which would fairly represent the time and labor expended by the producer, and who would be able to reject work that did not meet the standard set, the value of the goods would be increased. An equally necessary step in this matter would be the providing of a regular market for the goods and the supervision of production, so that the market would not be overloaded with certain articles and lacking in others. Experiments already carried out have proved the existence of a market for Porto Rican goods in the United States, and the matter should be taken up under the supervision of the Insular Government.

In order to produce trained workers for the production of these articles, it would be necessary to establish schools for their instruction which might well be under the direction of the Department of Education. These schools would not necessarily last throughout the year, nor would they require any great expenditure of money for their maintenance. The character of the school should depend upon the locality in which it was established and should be designed only for the training of skilled workmen, either child or adult, in particular lines of work. Short courses of two or three months in these industrial schools should be offered, and the people who attend them should be assured of a market for their goods when they have arrived at a point where they can produce goods of the proper standard. The money expended in the establishment and maintenance of these schools would more than double the earning capacity of the unskilled worker, and the general welfare of the community would be increased by the changing of unskilled and unproductive citizens into trained, productive laborers.

It is a well established fact that the trained workman is the most desirable kind of citizen. The unskilled laborer has no steady market for his labor and is the first victim in the wage system whenever a financial crisis causes the employer to lessen his expenses. The unskilled laborer has for sale a product which the average employer is not anxious to obtain, whereas the skilled worker can find a much more steady and regular market for his labor. The lawless, irresponsible class of citizens in any community is always composed to a great extent of the unskilled laborers, and any country which has an overwhelming proportion of its population composed of this class of people is in constant danger of labor disturbances and conflicts between employers and employees. The great majority of the men in penal institutions are unskilled laborers, and if the proportion of this type of citizens is sufficiently large, it may constitute a real danger to the community. With increased ability to earn wages comes the desire to improve living conditions and to rise higher in the social scale. This demands added education, more hygienic surroundings, and better food and clothing. The man who earns fifty cents a day, and that at irregular periods, is an early victim to dissatisfaction and is easily made to believe that life has not much for him in the future, and that he has not been fairly treated by his employer. The skilled laborer who earns double this amount or more, begins to take a new interest in life, as he can see the results which have come from his directed efforts, and values the benefit to his family; he educates his children, sees to it that they are well clothed and fed, and he himself becomes interested in the life and problems of the community as he becomes gradually a person of some importance in its economic and social life. A dependent wage-earning population usually lacks ideals of self-improvement, but the steady-working, independent producer of marketable goods is constantly striving to improve the amount and quality of his products.

THE LAND PROBLEM AND UNEMPLOYMENT

ONE of the most difficult problems to solve in the case of a small country such as Porto Rico, and one which has a definite bearing on both the economic and the social life of the people, is the land situation. This is especially true when the chief industries are such as lend themselves more readily to large plantation farming rather than to small industries or crops which can be raised profitably on small areas. The most important products of Porto Rico to-day are large-farm products, and they naturally tend to develop a small number of large landowners and a large number of landless citizens. There were in 1910, 46,799 farms operated by their owners, and it was estimated that 600,000 people or 117,647 families in rural sections belonged to the landless class. An equally large proportion of landless citizens is found in urban centers. Of the 10,936 people in Puerta de Tierra in 1913, only 178 or about 30 families owned the land on which their houses were located. It is estimated that there are at least 800,000 people or 156,860 landless families in Porto Rico.

In addition to the tendency toward lawlessness that is always found where there is an overproportion of landless citizens, the systems of land rental in Porto Rico have certain unfortunate economic aspects which call for consideration. Part of the renters live in houses which are owned by the proprietor of the land upon which their houses are located, and here the case resolves itself simply into the ordinary relations of renters and householders. This system does not differ to any great extent from the ordinary rent system in the States and has the same disadvantages, both economical and social, which are to be found wherever the rental system is in operation.

A second system which has been known as the "Land Rent System" is somewhat different. Under this system a man rents a lot from the owner of the property and proceeds to erect his own house upon the land. He then owns the house but not the land upon which it is located. Usually he rents from the proprietor from month to month or from year to year and has no definite lease of the land, and there is nothing to prevent the owner from raising the rental price or from demanding the house of the renter whenever he feels so inclined. As a matter of fact, it frequently happens that the land is rented to householders at fifty cents or a dollar monthly for the purpose of building houses, and within a short time after the completion of the house the owner of the land advances the price of rent, so that the house owner finds himself unable to meet the increased cost. He then has no choice except to move out and leave his house, together with the amount of work and invested money which it represents, or to sell the house to another person. Usually the house is sold to the owner of the land himself, who thus comes into possession, at a very reduced price, of a house which he, in turn, rents to another individual. This system is extremely unfortunate for the renter and should be abolished by the passing of legislation which would require the granting of a lease for a certain definite period to every person who builds upon land owned by another.

A modification of this system is frequently found in the cases where employees build their houses upon the land which belongs to the plantation. In many cases the employer does his utmost to make the life of his tenants as pleasant as possible, granting them garden plots and trying to make them permanent employees by offering them certain advantages. In many cases, however, the employer maintains a company store and requires his employees to purchase all their provisions from the store, thus making a double profit from them, and frequently charging them higher prices than they would have to pay elsewhere. In other cases the employer guarantees the credit of his workmen at a given local store, and on pay day he turns over to the local storekeeper the amount due the workmen and the storekeeper deducts from this the amount which is owing him for provisions and hands over to the workmen what may be left. As the average countryman has little idea of business and is lacking in knowledge of how to keep accurate accounts, and, moreover, since a credit system always tends to extravagance, it frequently happens that the workman is never entirely out of debt. There is a law approved in 1908 which makes it unlawful "for any corporation, company, firm or person engaged in any trade or business, whether directly or indirectly, to issue, sell, give or deliver to any person employed by such corporation, company, firm or person, payments of wages to such laborers, or as an advance for labor not due, in any script, token, draft, check or other evidence of indebtedness payable or redeemable otherwise than in lawful money." Section 2 of the same law provides that "if any corporation, company, firm or person shall coerce or compel or attempt to coerce or compel an employee to purchase goods or supplies in payment of wages due him from any corporation, company, firm or person, such said named corporation, company, firm or person shall be guilty of a misdemeanor." In this way attempts have been made to protect the laborer from exploitation, but violations of the law are not uncommon.

There is need for legislation to provide opportunity for the man of small means to purchase sufficient land to establish a home. In Porto Rico there are about 121,346 acres of government lands located in various parts of the Island which might well be opened to settlement at a nominal price. Legislation should also be passed which would provide that private land which is not used for produce for a given term of years might be opened to settlement and sold to people who would occupy it and use it for production. There are many acres of private land in Porto Rico which are not used at all and have not been used for years. The accumulation of land by an individual or a corporation for purposes of speculation or for purposes other than cultivation and use for the production of crops should be discouraged, because the limited amount of land in the Island does not permit such accumulation except at the expense of the poorer class of people. There is at present a law preventing the accumulation of more than 500 acres of land by any company or corporation, but no penalty has been provided for the violation of this law, and it is practically useless as it stands at present.

In addition to providing means by which people would be encouraged to own and manage small farms, coöperative organizations for providing a market for the products of these farms should be established. Undoubtedly, the government should start such a movement. The spirit of coöperation is not strong in Porto Rico at the present time, and the small farm holder finds himself at a disadvantage when he has to compete with the larger producer and when he is obliged to find a market for his goods. Some such system as exists in Denmark, where the farmers of a community have joined themselves into coöperative associations for selling their products and the purchase of necessary supplies, might very well be introduced into Porto Rico. This would tend not only to improve the economic situation by bringing better prices and a steady market for the farm products, and by making possible the purchase of necessary supplies in larger quantities, but it would also help to encourage a sense of unity and mutual confidence among the people of a given community, which would be of immense value in raising the standard of citizenship. Community pride and a definite desire for improvement would necessarily follow such a movement.

Farming is one of the few occupations which is not influenced by seasons, so far as unemployment is concerned. Practically all of the trades have their busy seasons and their idle seasons, and any movement which would tend to make employment more permanent by providing small farms for a larger number of people, would be of immense benefit to the Island as a whole. The Bureau of Labor of Porto Rico in an investigation which covered the last five months of the year 1913, found that of the total number of union men reported, 27 per cent were unemployed during the month of August, 26 per cent during September, 38 per cent during October, 34 per cent during November, and 46 per cent during December. The men reporting were engaged in various occupations. It was estimated that 28 per cent of all the laborers who reported were unemployed on account of lack of work and not on account of not desiring work. The different trades represented are as follows: among the dock laborers 62 per cent were unemployed, 56 per cent of the carpenters, 47 per cent of the agricultural laborers, 23 per cent of the cigar makers, and 10 per cent of the typesetters reported that they could not find employment. Thus it will be seen that when the individual workman is at the mercy of the employer, he has no independent status such as he would have were he the owner of even a very modest piece of property, and it is inevitable that he will find employment only part of the year. Part time employment tends to low standards of living, because during the period of reduced financial income the standards of living are lowered, and when it is found that the family can exist on the reduced income there is little inducement for seeking work since the desire for economy and saving is not greatly developed among the working classes of Porto Rico.

We find a gradual lowering of the moral standard as the necessary accompaniment of low standards of living, and if continued long enough, this low moral standard gradually leads to moral and social degeneration. The necessary steps should be taken by the legislature to provide for the relief of the landless and unemployed classes, as otherwise these people will constitute a serious handicap for the economic and social development of a competent body of citizens.

POVERTY

THE meaning of the word poverty is relative and depends upon the class of people to whom the word is applied. Poverty, technically, is the lack of an income sufficient to maintain the individual as the society in which he lives demands that he should live. Thus a wealthy man may live in relative poverty if he is in a circle of acquaintances who are much more wealthy than he is. The amount of income necessary to keep one from being classed in the poverty-stricken group decreases with the simplicity of individual, family, and community life. The amount of property necessary to keep one from poverty in the country is not as great as the amount of property necessary to keep one from poverty in the cities, due to the fact that the standards of living in the country are much simpler and require less expenditure of money to conform to the social standards. Pauperism is not the same as poverty. Poverty may be only temporary, depending upon unfavorable conditions which have reduced the income of the family, such as sickness, accident, lack of employment, or other factors beyond the control of the individual. Poverty does not necessarily involve any moral degeneration, while the pauper is entirely dependent on society and is a moral degenerate. Poverty, in general, however, is a dangerous condition, because it generally leads to pauperism. Poverty perpetuates itself if not taken care of; and if the poor man should give up the struggle against poverty, the general effect on society would be injurious, because, through contact, standards of living, social disease, and bad morals are contagious.

The competition between capital and labor, which often leads to poverty, is not fair if it is limited to the individual members of society. As the individual capitalist has more influence than the individual laborer, labor must be organized in order to equalize the situation. The competitive process between capital and labor, and between industrial organizations, should be controlled so that people should not be compelled to compete on an unfair basis.

The existing conditions in any community are largely responsible for poverty and often for pauperism. They are especially responsible for the attitude of the individual in regard to poverty as to whether he will make a fight to gain a place in society above the poverty-stricken class, or whether he simply resigns himself to his fate and continues to live in a poverty-stricken condition. In this situation, the well-to-do class is more responsible for poverty than any other class, because they have the most power, both legislative and moral, and they must assume for this reason a greater share of responsibility regarding the conditions in any given community. Poverty can be alleviated, but probably not entirely eliminated, and some of the means of combating poverty are the following:

First.—Education. By this means the efficiency of the individual in adjusting himself to trade environment is increased.

Second.—The self-support of weaker classes through voluntary associations among themselves, such as labor movements.

Third.—The proper kind of legal protection, such as factory, and woman and child labor laws, safeguards in factory work, the minimum wage, and accident laws.

Fourth.—Rational charity, by which cases of unusual necessity can be cared for. This charity should act as a temporary agency and should not become permanent, as in that case it tends to pauperism.

Fifth.—Eugenics, by which the physically and mentally unfit, who contribute largely to the pauper class, may be eliminated from society and prevented from propagating a second generation.

Modern charity is more democratic than older charity, and in its workings material aid is made subordinate to moral aid. It is optimistic and believes that radical improvements in social conditions are possible. It believes that the family should always be a self-supporting group, that charity should try to make the poverty-stricken family self-supporting, and that the family should be kept together.

One of the improvements in modern charity is what is known as organized charity, which is a sort of clearing house for the charities of a community. Organized charity does not extend material aid so much as it attempts to find work for needy individuals and thus do away with poverty by putting the family on a self-supporting basis. Organized charity would do away with the begging pauper and require him to present his case at the headquarters of the society, where an investigation of the necessities of his particular case could be made and an effort to find suitable employment for him undertaken. The individual who wished to contribute to charity would contribute to the central organization instead of to the wandering beggar. This would have two distinct benefits to society, as it would prevent the disagreeable sights often encountered where begging is allowed in public, and it would prevent the individual member of society from being imposed upon by a beggar who might be in sufficiently good physical condition to undertake work which would bring in enough to maintain himself and his family.

The question of organized charity in Porto Rico has been suggested at different times, but it has never met with any great popular response, due to the customs and traditions of a charity-giving people. The Island to-day has a large number of paupers who are entirely dependent upon the charity which they receive through begging, and the custom of giving in response to the requests of these beggars is so widespread, that at the present time organized charity would have a most difficult field of work to undertake.

The Island of Porto Rico is prosperous. In the last fiscal year there was a surplus of about $15,000,000 of exports over the imports into the Island; but the distribution of wealth in Porto Rico is not equalized. It has been estimated that the wealth of the Island is in the hands of about 15 per cent of the population, and that the remaining 85 per cent are practically dependent upon uncertain labor and wage conditions for their maintenance. The per capita wealth of a country determines to a great degree the financial situation as far as the average individual is concerned. From the following list of per capita wealth in some of the leading countries, it will be possible to estimate how the average Porto Rican compares with the average citizen of other countries in this regard. The following list is based on statistics of 1909:

Great Britain—	per capita wealth	$1,442
France	" " "	1,257
Australia	" " "	1,228
United States	" " "	1,123
Denmark	" " "	1,104
Canada	" " "	949
Belgium	" " "	734
Germany	" " "	707
Spain	" " "	548
Austria Hungary	" " "	499
Greece	" " "	485
Italy	" " "	485
Portugal	" " "	417

| Russia | " | " | " | 296 |
| Porto Rico | " | " | " | 182 |

From the above table it will be seen that the average individual in Porto Rico is comparatively poor.

The economic situation in Porto Rico is giving rise to the formation of classes based on wealth. With the introduction of available markets and modern methods of commerce and industry which followed the American occupation, the land values rapidly increased. The small landholder, seeing the increase in price which came about and believing that it was to his best advantage to sell his land, disposed of it to the representatives of large landholding concerns for what, to him, was a fabulous price. As soon as the money from this sale was expended, the original landholder found himself absolutely dependent upon the mercy of a wage-paying employer. In this way a great part of small landholdings passed into the hands of representatives of large landholdings and caused the formation of the two groups, the capitalistic group, which is limited to a comparatively small number of people, and the wage-earning group, which comprises probably 90 per cent of the population of Porto Rico. As a result we lack in Porto Rico the great middle class of financially independent farmers which constitutes the strength of the United States and the more prosperous European countries. A serious and systematic effort to build up a prosperous and independent middle class, either by encouraging small-farm or other industries, is necessary if the majority of the people are to attain the advantages which they should enjoy, and if the social and economic status of the Island is to be made equitable and stable.

The reduced wage system and the absolute dependence of the wage-earning group has given rise to a great many labor disturbances within the last few years. These labor disturbances have included both city and country groups and have in nearly all cases been caused by an effort to better the working conditions and to secure an increase of wages. In the great majority of the cases there is no doubt but that the laborers were justified in asking for better conditions than those which actually existed. That the disturbances sometimes ended in riots and led to the destruction of property is the fault of the educational condition of the people, who are easily excited and led to believe that only by the use of violence can they secure the things which they demand.

The relation between poverty and health and poverty and morals is very close. The poverty-stricken family cannot be led to take any great amount of interest in society or health betterment until means have been produced by which the economic situation of the family group can be bettered. The expense of living uses up the daily wage of the ordinary unskilled laborer in Porto Rico, who averages fifty or sixty cents per day for the time that the weather and his physical condition permit him to work. There is also a close relation between sickness and poverty, the average countryman of Porto Rico being only partly as efficient a worker as he should be, due to physical weakness caused by anemia or malaria. Poverty is closely related to degeneration and crime, especially when it descends into pauperism and absolute dependence upon charity.

The climate and geographical conditions of Porto Rico have never provided the laborer with any incentive to economize, inasmuch as he has no need for providing against a period of cold, and Nature produces some form of plant or vegetable food throughout the entire year. Clothing and lodging may be of the simplest and still prevent much suffering under such conditions, and with physical weakness caused by disease, the tendency is to live for the present, and to take little care for the future through a system of saving and economy. The average manual laborer saves nothing and makes little effort to accumulate property. Incentive must be provided through education which will accustom the countryman to the idea of accumulation of property in a small way, so that dependence upon charity will not be necessary in the case of a financial or economic crisis. That there is a movement toward saving is evident from the fact that on June 30, 1915, there were savings accounts to the amount of $1,909,969.34 in the various banks in the Island. This, however, is a comparatively small amount, and the younger generation should be given definite instruction and incentives along the line of savings. The introduction of the Postal Savings Bank has been of great value in this respect, and the school savings banks have also done their share in inculcating the principles of economy.

SICKNESS AND DISEASE

THE Island of Porto Rico is more free from disease than the average tropical or semi-tropical country, due to the active efforts of the medical profession and of the special commissions and departments created for the elimination of disease within the last few years. Nevertheless, a great deal of sickness which might be avoided, part of which is responsible for death, and part of which merely incapacitates the sufferers or renders them less useful citizens, is to be found. The elimination of such diseases as smallpox and yellow fever, which formerly were responsible for a great number of deaths and which descended upon the Island as epidemics with considerable regularity, has been accomplished, and if similar care were taken in the case of less dreaded diseases, there is reason to believe that they could also be wiped out of existence in the Island.

For the year 1915-16 there was a total of 26,572 deaths in Porto Rico. Most of these deaths were from diseases classified as transmissible, and, consequently, from diseases which could be prevented by complete quarantine. Following is a list of the number of deaths from the diseases which took the heaviest toll in the Island:

Rickets	1,271
Tuberculosis (lungs)	2,125
Malaria	1,290
Typhoid fever	94
Whooping cough	167
Tetanus	109
Cancer	365
Meningitis	344
Epilepsy	57
Acute bronchitis	1,015

Chronic bronchitis	309
Bronco-pneumonia	822
Pneumonia	569
Diarrhea and enteritis under two years	3,485
Diarrhea and enteritis two years and over	870
Infantile tetanus	729
Lack of care in infancy	117
Congenital debility in children	1,145
Uncinariasis	479
Smallpox	9
Diphtheria	26

The two diseases which are of most vital importance to the people of Porto Rico at present are undoubtedly tuberculosis and anemia. The ravages of tuberculosis are more noticeable in the cities, and it has been stated that in 1912, on one street in San Juan, 12 out of every 100 residents died of this disease. Anemia is prevalent throughout the Island, but is more noticeable in the country districts than in the cities, and while the death rate for anemia is not so high as the death rate of some other diseases, yet by reason of weakening the vitality of the sufferers it tends to offer a fertile spot for the incubation of germs of other diseases, and the working and producing power of the individual is lessened with the acuteness of the disease.

It has been claimed that anemia was introduced into Porto Rico by the negroes who were brought here as slaves in the sixteenth and seventeenth centuries, and the identity of the disease with the anemia existing in about 20 per cent of all the negroes of the Gold Coast has been determined. The disease was for a long time limited to the coast land and was propagated on the sugar plantations, but after the introduction of coffee, which has come to be the chief product of the mountain regions, the disease was propagated throughout the entire Island.

This disease has left its trace among the country people and they have been accused of laziness and idleness when it is probable that the cause of the apparent disinclination for work is due to the weakened physical condition which is a result of the anemia. In this connection, Drs. Gutierrez and Ashford in their work on *Uncinariasis in Porto Rico* quote Col. George D. Flinter, an Englishman in the service of Spain, who published in 1834 "An account of Porto Rico," as follows:

"The common white people, or lowest class (called *jíbaros*), swing in their hammocks all day long, smoking cigars and scraping their native guitars.... Most of these colonists are inconceivably lazy and indifferent. Lying back in their hammocks, the entire day is passed praying or smoking. Their children, isolated from the cities, without education, live in social equality with the young negroes of both sexes, acquiring perverted customs, only to later become cruel with their slaves."

Commenting on this statement, Drs. Gutierrez and Ashford speak as follows:

"What if these people were merely innocent victims of a disease, modern only in name? What if the brand placed by the Spaniard, the Englishman, and the Frenchman in olden times upon the *jíbaro* of Porto Rico were a bitter injustice? The early reports savor strongly of those touristic impressions of the Island which from time to time crop out in the press of modern America, in which 'laziness and worthlessness' of the 'natives' are to be inferred, if, indeed, these very words are not employed to describe a sick workingman, with only half of the blood he should have in his body."

"True, Col. Flinter, Field Marshall Count O'Reilly, and the rest of the long list of early 'observers' did not know what uncinariasis was. But is it necessary that we have a record of microscopic examinations of the feces of the people they describe to realize what can be read between the lines? Convicts, adventurers, and gypsies may have formed part of the element that colonized Porto Rico, but we cannot believe that these were all, nor that their descendants were 'lazy' and 'worthless.'

"We cannot believe that vicious idleness comes natural to the Spanish colonist, even in the Tropics, for the very reason that we have seen these descendants at their very worst, after the neglect of four centuries by their mother country, and after the laborious increase of an anemic population in the face of a deadly disease, whose nature was neither known nor studied, work from sunrise to sunset and seek medical attention, not because they felt sick, but because they could no longer work.

"We strongly feel that these writers have unconsciously described uncinariasis. Are the Spanish people considered 'lazy' by those who know them? Were those Spaniards who conquered Mexico, Peru, and all South

America, who formed so formidable a power in the Middle Ages, a lazy people?

"Is it 'laziness' or disease that is this very day attracting the attention of the United States to the descendant of the pure-blooded English stock in the Southern Appalachian Range, in the mountains of Carolina and Tennessee, the section of our country where the greatest predominance of 'pure American blood' occurs, despised by the negro who calls him 'poor white trash'?"

During the year 1914-15 there were 6,644 deaths of children under two years of age, which constituted 28.8 per cent of the total mortality of the Island. Approximately 14 out of every 100 children born, died in infancy, and the death rate for the total population was 5.55 per cent for children under one year of age, and 7.71 per cent for children under two years of age. Diarrhea and enteritis were responsible for 33.8 per cent of infant mortality; congenital debility for 13.14 per cent; infantile tetanus for 10.32; while disease of the respiratory organs caused 16.17 per cent of the infant mortality.

It has never been definitely determined just what losses, from the point of view of days of labor, or from the point of view of vitality of the laborer, have been caused by malaria. Mr. D. L. Van Dine, in an article in the *Southern Medical Journal* for March, 1915, gives the result of some of his investigations among the laboring class in Louisiana. In this study, which was made on one of the large plantations and which covered 74 tenant families with a total of 299 individuals, he shows the losses which occurred from May to October 15, 1914. There were 970 days of actual illness of such a nature that the illness was reported to the physician. Forty-eight out of the seventy-four families were reported to the doctor for malaria. According to Mr. Van Dine, this does not take into consideration mild attacks of malaria which were not reported to the physician, especially in the cases of children. He has estimated that there were at least 487 days lost in cases which were not reported to the doctor. He also estimates that there was a loss of 385 days on the part of the adults who assisted in caring for the malaria patients. It is estimated that there was a loss in days of labor equal to nearly six days and a half for each case of malaria. It will easily be seen that this may be a serious loss of time as far as the production of crops is concerned, and even thus it does not fairly represent the loss, as it does not take into consideration the weakened energy of the man just before or just after the malarial attack.

Undoubtedly, there is as great a loss in Porto Rico from malaria as is indicated in the statements just made. It has been reported that in some sections of the Island, 85 per cent of the people were found to have malaria germs in their blood. Between the two diseases of malaria and anemia, there is no doubt that the physical condition of the Porto Rican countrymen is gradually debilitated.

Since the American occupation, stress has been laid upon the attempts to eliminate anemia, and this work has received special attention since 1906. During the year 1914-15 there were 32,278 new cases of anemia treated in different parts of the Island, and 15,497 cases were discharged as cured.

Undoubtedly a great deal of the illness in Porto Rico is the result of improper food, or food prepared in an improper manner. Malnutrition among children is frequent and leads to such diseases as rickets, which we find has an exceptionally high death rate. In the recent measurements given at the University among university students, it has been found that there was an average depth of chest of nearly half an inch more than is found in the American boy or girl of the same age, and this has been considered as an indication of malnutrition and general softening of the bones in early childhood.

A hemoglobin test which was given to the students of the University this year showed that the average among the men was 80.04 per cent, and only 77.6 per cent among the women. The average for Porto Rico should not fall below 85 per cent, and the anemic conditions indicated by the low average is an indication that the disease is to be found not only among the country people, but also among people of the best conditions of life.

It will be impossible to settle the economic and social problems of Porto Rico until the question of personal health has been more nearly solved than it is to-day. With a large proportion of the country people sick from anemia and malaria, and with tuberculosis as prevalent as it is at the present time, the weakened vitality will not permit strenuous or continued work sufficient to improve economic conditions to any great extent. Social conditions, depending as they do upon the economic situation, must also be slow of improvement, and the most important work facing the Government of Porto Rico at present is the elimination of such diseases as impair the physical condition of the people and thus interfere with economic and social progress.

CRIME

GENERALLY speaking, criminals may be divided into three classes: first, those who direct crime but who take no active part in the commission of the crime themselves; second, those who commit crimes which require a considerable amount of personal courage; third, those who commit crimes which do not necessarily involve any great amount of personal courage. There might be added a fourth class, which would consist of those who commit crime through ignorance of the law or carelessness in informing themselves of exact legal measures and in heeding this knowledge when once obtained. During the year 1915-16 there was a total of 53,006 arrests in the Island of Porto Rico. Of this number, nearly 47,000 were men and the rest were women. On the basis of a population of 1,200,000, this would give one arrest for every 22 persons in the Island. Of this total number of arrests, however, only 438 were cases of felony. There were a great many arrests for the infraction of municipal ordinances,—something over 11,000 in all,—and more than 8,000 arrests for disturbance of the peace. Over 9,000 were for gambling, and over 2,000 for petty larceny; about 5,000 arrests were for infraction of the sanitary laws, and nearly 2,000 arrests were for infraction of road laws. This shows that the greater number of arrests was for comparatively unimportant crimes; by unimportant meaning, of course, those crimes which do not directly involve the loss of life or of any great amount of property. The felonies committed during the year were as follows:

Murders	41
Homicides	26
Attempt at murder	30
Robbery	5
Rape	15
Seduction	24
Crime against nature	3
Arson	5
Burglary	148

Forgery	6
Counterfeiting	1
Grand larceny	10
Cattle stealing	25
Smuggling	5
Extortion	2
Crime against the public health and security	55
Mayhem	11
Violation of postal laws	5
Violation of graves	1
Conspiracy	8
Falsification	7

giving a total of 438, which includes not only those sentenced but also those indicted and acquitted. From this table it will be seen that a relatively small number of the actual felonies committed are felonies involving loss of life or an attempt against life. In support of this table, and in proof of the fact that crimes of violence are relatively few in Porto Rico, the following table is given, which is a record of the convictions of the district courts of the Island of Porto Rico in criminal cases, for the years 1913-14 and 1914-15, and of the convicts in the penitentiary June 30, 1915:

	Number of convictions		Percentage of crimes		In penitentiary	Per cent in prison
	1913-14	1914-15	1913-14	1914-15		
Violation of laws enacted in	220	842	.23	.45	142	.10

exercise
of police
powers

Against persons	286	432	.30	.23	371	.25
Against property	329	312	.34	.17	779	.53
Against the administration of public justice	29	142	.03	.08	21	.01
Against decency	40	51	.04	.03	97	.06
Against good morals	36	35	.04	.02	20	.01
Against reputation	9	16	.01	.01	...	..
Unclassified	10	7	.01	.01	38	.03
	----	-----			-----	
Totals	959	1,837			1,468	

From the above table it will be seen that crimes against persons constitute 23 to 30 per cent of the crimes committed. Of the total number of convicts in the penitentiary for the commission of crime, 25 per cent, during the year 1914-15, were there for crimes against persons. Thus we may definitely state that about 25 per cent of the crimes carried to the district courts of Porto Rico are those which involve attempts against the life or well-being of another person. It will be noticed from the above table that with few exceptions the percentages of crimes for the two years are very nearly equal. In 1913-14, 34 per cent of the crimes were against property, which was not strange when we consider that this was a year of financial crisis, due to the sugar situation. In the same year 23 per cent of the crimes were in violation of laws enacted in exercise of police powers. These crimes included breach of the peace.

In the following year, 1914-15, when we had about 17,000 laborers engaged in strikes throughout the Island, and when in addition to this there was a general Insular election, we find that the number of crimes against property dropped to 17 per cent, whereas the number of crimes in violation of laws enacted in exercise of police powers rose from 23 per cent to 45 per cent. This would tend to prove that the average lawbreaker in Porto Rico is easily influenced by economic circumstances and by social surroundings, and that at such a period as that of strikes or elections criminal tendencies take the direction of breach of the peace and violation of municipal ordinances, rather than such crimes as arson, burglary, embezzlement, or forgery.

The influence of the election year is also noticeable in the group of crimes prejudicial to the administration of public justice, which includes contempt of court, bribery, and perjury. During the year 1913-14, 3 per cent of the convictions fell under this head, while during the year 1914-15, the amount was 8 per cent. It will be noticed that of the prisoners in the penitentiary the percentage of those convicted for violation of laws enacted in exercise of police power is only 10 per cent, much less than the percentage of those convicted in the district courts. This, of course, is accounted for by the fact that the great majority of violations of these laws are punishable by fines rather than by imprisonment. In the same way, the percentage of prisoners for crimes against property is much larger than the percentage of convictions in the district courts for this crime, due, of course, to the fact that these crimes are more frequently punished by a prison sentence than by a fine, thus giving an accumulation from year to year of convicts, which overbalances the per cent of the court convictions for any single year.

According to the report of the Insular Chief of Police, the town which had the greatest number of arrests, in proportion to its population, for the year 1915-16, was Arroyo, where there was one arrest for every 8.47 persons. This was followed by Salinas, with one arrest for every 8.82 persons. The town with the best record was Las Marías, where there was one arrest for every 162.03 persons. On the basis of the records of the municipal courts for the three years of 1912-13, 1913-14, and 1914-15, the judicial districts stand in the following relation as far as the number of criminal cases presented during that time is concerned. The table given shows one criminal case presented every three years for the number of inhabitants indicated in each judicial district.

San Juan   one case for every 17.79 persons

Rio Piedras	"	"	"	"	18.42	"
Patillas	"	"	"	"	19.94	"
Vieques	"	"	"	"	19.98	"
Salinas	"	"	"	"	23.34	"
Guayama	"	"	"	"	24.62	"
Yauco	"	"	"	"	24.14	"
Mayaguez	"	"	"	"	27.50	"
Vega Baja	"	"	"	"	28.74	"
Humacao	"	"	"	"	27.31	"
San Lorenzo	"	"	"	"	30.66	"
Ciales	"	"	"	"	31.07	"
Fajardo	"	"	"	"	31.40	"
Juana Diaz	"	"	"	"	33.00	"
Cáguas	"	"	"	"	33.01	"
Yabucoa	"	"	"	"	33.24	"
Añasco	"	"	"	"	36.29	"
Ponce	"	"	"	"	36.92	"
Manatí	"	"	"	"	37.89	"
Arecibo	"	"	"	"	38.23	"
Cayey	"	"	"	"	38.29	"
Lares	"	"	"	"	40.83	"
Rio Grande	"	"	"	"	40.90	"
Barros	"	"	"	"	41.09	"

Bayamón	"	"	"	"	43.87	"
San Germán	"	"	"	"	44.70	"
Adjuntas	"	"	"	"	44.97	"
Coamo	"	"	"	"	45.19	"
Camuy	"	"	"	"	47.13	"
San Sebastián	"	"	"	"	48.55	"
Aguadilla	"	"	"	"	50.22	"
Utuado	"	"	"	"	54.61	"
Carolina	"	"	"	"	57.63	"
Cabo Rojo	"	"	"	"	64.99	"

The great proportion of crime in San Juan, as compared with the rest of the Island, is of course largely due to social conditions, inasmuch as it is the largest city in the Island and to a great extent the resort of undesirable characters for this reason. In the second place, as a coast town and the most important shipping and commercial center, it has a more or less shifting population, and a population composed to a great extent of an uneducated type among the working classes. Every seaport town offers opportunities for criminal classes which inland towns do not possess. The second town in the list, Rio Piedras, is the natural outlet between San Juan and the rest of the Island, which undoubtedly accounts for its large percentage of crime. The rest of the towns where crime is found in large proportion will be discovered to have a large floating population, people who are day laborers and who have no particular interest in the community, except as it provides them with an opportunity for earning daily wages. This class of population is always unfavorable to a community and is always to be found where large industries exist which employ a great number of men; and this is especially true when little attempt is made on the part of the employer to render the permanence of the job desirable by furnishing well-provided living facilities for the employee. It is noticeable that in Cabo Rojo, where the percentage of criminal cases is lowest, the population depends chiefly upon the hat-making industry for its support. This is added proof of the value of small industries from the point of view of community welfare.

It is noteworthy that there was an immense increase in the number of crimes committed in the following districts: Ciales, where the number of cases increased from 431 in 1912 to 754 in 1915; Lares, where the increase was from 352 to 853; Vieques, where the increase was from 341 to 684; Yabucoa, where the increase was from 589 to 831; Yauco, where the increase was from 867 to 1,490. In the rest of the districts the number of crimes did not vary greatly from year to year, even decreasing in the case of Rio Piedras from 1,101 in 1912 to 911 in 1915. Of course, the difference in crime percentage might depend upon the efficiency of the police force or upon the severity of the Municipal Judge, but undoubtedly it will be found more often to depend upon local conditions such as strikes, or the introduction of large numbers of workingmen from another district to take part in agricultural or industrial work. The change of location and the resulting necessity of accommodation to local surroundings is apt to be dangerous to the morals of the individual.

The great majority of the arrests were for crimes which would be termed city crimes. The average countryman of Porto Rico is a man who has a great deal of respect for the law and is inclined to obey it unless led into trouble in a moment of passion or while under the influence of alcoholic drinks. Throughout the country districts premeditated crime is rare, and from the standpoint of improvement of the community, the cities and large towns should be the chief points of attack. A great deal of carelessness exists as to complying with local laws and municipal ordinances, and it is estimated that on June 30, 1915, there were confined in the Insular jails and detention houses, prisoners in the relation of one to every 7.17 inhabitants of the Island. The chief work of the schools along the line of prevention of crime should be the explanation of laws, both Insular and municipal, and the explanation of the reasons for such laws, in order that the individual may be led by his own volition to avoid lawbreaking. Parents should also be impressed with the necessity of inculcating in their children a respect for constituted authority and the necessary obedience to it in order that as the children develop into men and women they may have the proper respect for the laws and those who have been appointed to enforce them.

INTEMPERANCE

IT is unnecessary to say anything about the evil effects of the use of alcoholic drinks, whether it be from the physical, moral, or economic point of view. The recent agitation in favor of the prohibition of the manufacture and sale of alcoholic beverages in Porto Rico, however, has caused more discussion regarding the situation here than has ever before been the case, and a brief statement of facts may not be unwarranted.

The Porto Ricans are not given to the overconsumption of alcoholic drinks. They are not heavy drinkers, and drunkenness is not at all common. Probably every village has its unfortunate inhabitants, few in number, who live usually under the influence of intoxicants. But the great majority of the people are not given to the excessive use of alcohol. The use of wines is common, a custom characteristic of most Latin peoples.

Porto Rico produces a great deal of alcohol, it being one of the by-products of the sugar cane. Data are not available to show just how much of the rum and alcohol produced is used in the Island, and how much is exported, or how much is used for drinking purposes and how much for commercial uses. During the fiscal year 1915-16, a total revenue of $1,111,834.30 was paid to the Insular government on alcoholic liquors manufactured in Porto Rico or imported into the Island. This gives a per capita revenue of nearly one dollar, and this revenue was paid on 3,886,705 liters of alcoholic liquors either manufactured here or imported—a per capita allowance of more than three liters for every inhabitant of the Island. It is probably true that a great deal of the alcohol manufactured in Porto Rico was exported, but even granting that one half was not used here, the amount of one and a half liters for every inhabitant is excessive.

The average grocery store carries a complete line of bottled drinks, and often beer in the keg, as well. This is one of the first things which impresses the visitor from the States when he enters a grocery store and sees the shelves packed with all kinds of bottles. There is a constant sale for goods of this sort, usually to the workingmen and poorer class of people, who purchase in small quantities, a drink at a time, for three or five cents; many of them, no doubt, attempting to keep up their physical strength by the use of such a stimulant, since a more noticeable stimulating effect is produced by five cents' worth of rum than could be obtained through the consumption of five cents' worth of food. When this custom becomes as prevalent as it is in Porto Rico, it involves serious evil effects.

There are few drug users in the Island, and the strict enforcement of the Harrison Drug Law will prevent drug using from becoming the menace to health and morals to the extent that we find to be the case in many of the cities of the United States. There is, however, a large quantity of patent medicines used, many of which have a sufficient amount of alcohol or narcotic drug element to render them dangerous from the point of view of habit formation.

Many of the poorer people do not have the money to pay the fees of a doctor and to purchase at a drug store the medicine which he prescribes. Moreover, many medical men do not listen with as much patience as they might, to the detailed list of complaints which the countryman has to offer. As a consequence, the countryman buys a bottle of medicine which has been recommended to him by a friend, or perhaps by the druggist, who often serves as a consulting physician in the smaller towns. If the medicine makes him feel better, he becomes a firm believer in its power to cure. Whether the result produced is actually a bettering of his physical condition, or merely a deadening of the nerves by means of a narcotic, he does not stop to ask. He recommends the medicine to his friends as a sure remedy for all their illnesses, and probably makes of it a household remedy, to be used by all members of the family when they feel indisposed. The author has known of many instances in which medicine has been purchased from patent medicine firms in the States, because of advertisements in the newspapers, and of several cases, where the money was returned by federal authorities with the statement that the company addressed had been closed by the post office authorities because it was found that their claims were not legitimate and that their medicines were valueless. The average Porto Rican places a great deal of confidence in what he reads in the news papers, and the papers are not as careful as they should be regarding the question of admitting advertising matter.

There is no great amount of public opinion against the use of alcohol in Porto Rico, and until, through the schools, the press, or some other agency, the people as a whole can be brought to see the disadvantage of its use, there can be but little accomplished in the direction of temperance and prohibition. The prohibition movement in the United States is not a matter of the moment alone, it is a movement which has been growing for years, and at the present time seems to have the majority of the population behind it. This is not the case in Porto Rico, and it is doubtful whether an abrupt change, unless backed up by strong public opinion, and the authority of the great majority of the people, would accomplish much in the way of betterment of conditions.

JUVENILE DELINQUENTS

ONE of the most difficult problems that faces organized society to-day is the disposal of delinquent children, and in order to meet this problem, the Juvenile Court system has been established in the United States, and by a law approved March 11, 1915, the Juvenile Court system was introduced into Porto Rico to take effect on June 1, 1915.

Up to within recent times juvenile offenders have been subjected to the same laws and the same penalties as hardened criminals, and there is no doubt but that a great many boys and girls who had broken some law or local ordinance, often through carelessness or ignorance, were placed in detention houses with older criminals and in this way became accustomed to the criminal classes and frequently were induced to enter upon a life of crime.

The prevailing idea of criminal law is to punish the offender for the offense committed against the laws of the state. Modern social science teaches that it is unfair to boys or girls of tender age to visit a punishment of this sort upon them, especially when it may lead to a continuance of crime, rather than to an avoidance of it in the future. Consequently, with the introduction of the Juvenile Court system the cases are taken out of criminal procedure and placed under the jurisdiction of courts of equity. The trials are usually informal, although the child has a right to a trial by jury in case he is accused of a serious offense, and he has the right to legal counsel, if he so desires. These rights, however, are very seldom exercised, inasmuch as it is coming to be recognized that the judges represent an actual attempt to do what is best for the child and do not represent in any way the prosecuting power of the state.

The principal figure in a Juvenile Court is the judge of the court, and wherever it is possible to do so, men especially trained in juvenile psychology should be appointed to this office. A knowledge of children and an understanding and appreciation of their feelings is necessary on the part of the judge, and he should be a person of sufficiently magnetic personality to win the sympathies of the children and to enable him to gain their confidence. To what an extent the influence of a single man may reach in the case of juvenile offenders and how far his influence may prevent crime among children, is well seen in the case of Judge Lindsey, of Denver, Colorado.

The second official in the court is the probation officer, who is under the authority of the judge, makes the necessary investigations when cases are reported to him, and presents the facts in the case to the judge of the court. He also must look after the children who have passed through the court to see that the sentences of the court are carried out; and if the children are placed on probation under the guardianship of relatives or friends, he must make visits sufficient in number and often enough so that he can be sure that the best interests of the child are being safeguarded, and if he finds the case to be otherwise, to report the facts to the judge of the court.

As the financial situation in Porto Rico did not permit the establishment of a completely new judicial system, it was decided to appoint the judge of each of the seven district courts of the Island to act as judge of the Juvenile Court. The prosecutors and municipal court judges are also probation officers *ex officio*, and the justices of the peace and others appointed by the district judges may be asked to serve as special probation officers. The Juvenile Courts in Porto Rico have original jurisdiction over juvenile offenders, and any case appealed from the Juvenile Courts may go directly to the Supreme Court of the Island. The courts are courts of record and the judges have authority to set the dates and places when and where sessions of the court will be held, to summon witnesses and compel them to appear in court. The jurisdiction of the Juvenile Courts in Porto Rico extends to all children under 16 years of age who are accused of any crime whatsoever, and it also applies to all people under 21 years of age, if they have ever been under the jurisdiction of the Juvenile Court before they were 16. The Juvenile Court also has jurisdiction over adults who have been responsible for the abandonment of children or who have contributed in any way to the delinquency of the child.

Of course, this situation is not an ideal one for the best working out of the problems that confront a Juvenile Court system. In the first place, it is practically impossible for men who act as criminal judges or criminal prosecutors to adopt the attitude so necessary for the fulfillment of the work of a juvenile court officer, as their training has been such as to influence them to believe that the prisoner is an offender and that violations of the law must be punished with sufficient severity to prevent a repetition of the offense on the part of the prisoner, and to serve as a warning for others who might be tempted to commit the same offense. The Juvenile Court officer, on the other hand, should regard only the best future interests of the child, and the question with him should not be as to whether a proper punishment may be inflicted for what the child has done, but as to how the future conduct of the child may be bettered after a due consideration of all the influences of heredity and environment in each particular case.

From July 1, 1915, to January 1, 1916, a total of 164 cases came before the Juvenile Courts. Of these, three cases were girls accused of petty larceny, and two were charged with being abandoned. The remaining 159 cases were boys. The cause given in nearly every case for the bad conduct of the children was one of the four following:

1. Lack of parental authority.
2. Bad environment.
3. Ignorance.
4. Poverty

Of the total number, 83 boys were accused of larceny, 25 were abandoned children, 18 were accused of fighting, 9 were accused of gambling, 7 were accused of breach of the peace, 4 were accused of attempts at larceny, 3 were accused of stoning buildings, and the rest were accused of various minor offenses.

An investigation of the home conditions of these boys brings out some pertinent facts in connection with the influence of a broken home upon the actions of the children. Of the total number of cases presented, 21 lived with their parents, 54 lived with their mothers, 23 lived with their fathers, and 22 lived with relatives, 13 lived with guardians, 13 had absolutely no homes and existed as best they might, with no permanent dwelling place, while 8 lived with friends. Thus we see that in the great majority of cases the children came from homes where they lacked the guidance and authority of at least one parent. Only 50 of the 164 had attended school, and only 15 had succeeded in passing the third grade in the public schools. Of the total number, 85 were illegitimate children, and 15 did not know whether their parents were married or not.

It is estimated that the city of San Juan alone has 500 homeless children and that there are at least 10,000 children in the Island who have absolutely no home and who are entirely without the influence of parental control. Doubtless, a great majority of these children are the result of illegitimate unions. What that means to the future of Porto Rico can very easily be imagined when we consider that they are growing up absolutely without control and without respect for authority of any sort. In very few cases do they at tend the public schools, and they must remain in this homeless condition, living as best they can, stealing or begging, when honest means of obtaining food do not avail. Thus they grow up learning the vice that can be found among the most poverty-stricken and criminal classes with whom they associate, and forming a group of people with criminal tendencies, and in their turn causing to be produced another generation of children who will be handicapped by the environment and the training which their fathers have received. The Government should colonize these homeless children on government lands where they may be taught a trade and where an attempt should be made to give them some idea of what life may mean to the educated, industrious citizen. The results would more than justify the necessary expenditure of money.

The Juvenile Court in Porto Rico has three means at its disposal for taking care of children that fall under its jurisdiction. It may send them to the Reform School at Mayaguez, in case they are boys. (There is no Reform School for girls in the Island.) It may also send them to one of the two charity schools in existence, or it may place them under the supervision of a friend or relative who must respond to the probation officer for their good conduct. The Reform School at Mayaguez will accommodate only 100 inmates, and as these are usually required to complete a rather long term of years in the institution, the number of vacancies occurring in the school each year is very small. The charity schools, both for boys and girls, are also overcrowded, and there is very little chance of the Juvenile Court being able to send any of its cases to either of these institutions. As a result, special wards have been prepared in the Insular penitentiary, and the most serious cases are assigned to these wards until such a time as there is a possibility of their being placed in the Reform School. An attempt is made to give the inmates of these special wards industrial work and some academic instruction, and they are kept absolutely separate from adult prisoners.

Of the 164 cases mentioned, the following disposition was made of the children: 34 were sent to correctional institutions (most of these were sent to the special wards in the penitentiary), 38 were placed under the care of their mothers, 24 were placed under the care of their fathers, 9 were placed under the care of both parents, 8 under the care of friends, 12 under the care of guardians, 17 under the care of relatives, and 6 were sent to the charity schools.

The problem of juvenile offenders is more acute in Porto Rico than in the United States, due to the fact that there are more opportunities open in Porto Rico for juvenile offenders than are to be found, possibly with the exception of the largest cities, in the United States. The early physical development of the tropics adds to the difficulties of the situation, and also the temptations that surround homeless children even at a comparatively early age. In addition to this, we have many instances of consensual marriages, which offer a temptation to even the very young to lower the standards of morality and to become careless regarding the marriage relation. The large number of poverty-stricken and homeless undoubtedly contributes a great deal to physical as well as mental and moral degeneration, and the combination of these factors may perhaps account for the large number of weak-minded and insane that we find at large in the majority of the towns of the Island.

In addition, promiscuous sexual relations undoubtedly contribute to this degeneracy, and if active steps are not taken to prepare these homeless children for better living and to enable them to earn an honest living, they will serve as the propagators of another generation of equally homeless, pauperized, and degenerate citizens.

RURAL SCHOOLS

ONE of the most perplexing problems which the Department of Education has to face in Porto Rico is the problem of the rural schools. In addition to a school budget too small to provide the number of rural schools necessary for all of the children of school age, there are added difficulties in the way of poverty and sickness among the country people which lead to irregular attendance on the part of the children, poor roads, and the keeping of children out of school in order to help earn money to support the family, especially in districts where child labor may be used profitably; and above all these difficulties is the great difficulty of furnishing the rural schools with teachers who are adequately trained and who have a comprehensive view of their mission as teachers and of the duty of the school to the community in which it is located.

The rural school problem will never be solved until we are able to provide teachers who are thoroughly prepared for the work which they have to do, and who look upon this work as being as important as any other profession. At present the rural school teachers fall into two rather large classes: first, the young, inexperienced, and often untrained teacher; and, second, the old, often out-of-date teacher, who has been unable to keep step with the progress of the town schools and has been pushed out into the country. Neither of these classes is fitted to give the best instruction in the rural schools; neither of them considers the position of a rural teacher as a permanent one, and in order to accomplish his best work the rural teacher should be expected to live in one community for a term of years so that he may fully understand and appreciate the problems of that community and become thoroughly acquainted with the patrons of his school.

The wages of the rural teacher should be such as will enable him to live in comfort, and as part of his wages the Government might very well assign him a parcel of land, together with living quarters, which would tend to make his residence in the district more permanent and which would enable him to carry on experimental work in agriculture at his own home.

There is no doubt but that the time will come when consolidated schools will be established in each *barrio* for the benefit of the children of the community. In this way, better teachers, better school buildings, better equipment, and a better arranged schedule of studies can be provided, as an untrained teacher who works with poor facilities and who has to handle two different groups of children in the day and who may have six grades to teach, is working under a disadvantage which greatly handicaps the work.

This is especially true when the teacher has no permanent interest in the rural school problem and regards his term of office there simply as a stepping-stone to a place in the graded school system of the town. In the annual report of the Commissioner of Education for 1914-15 we find the following data in regard to the rural schools of Porto Rico:

"The rural schools are located in the *barrios* or rural subdivisions of the municipalities. Of the 1,200,000 inhabitants which comprise the total population of the Island, about 79 per cent live in this rural area and about 70 per cent of them are illiterate. At the present time there are approximately 331,233 children of school age (between 5 and 18 years) living in the barrios. Of these only 91,966 or 27 per cent were enrolled in the rural schools at any time during the past year. This shows a decrease from the figures reported last year, but the fact is accounted for by an order issued from the central office prohibiting rural teachers from enrolling more than 80 pupils. In some of the populous barrios the teachers were enrolling 150 pupils and sometimes more. Inasmuch as neither the material conditions of the school buildings nor the professional equipment of the teachers justified such a burden, it was deemed wise, even in the face of an overwhelming school population for which no provision is made, to limit the enrollment to a size compatible with a semblance of efficiency. The average number of pupils belonging during the year to the rural schools was 76,341. The average number of teachers at work in these schools was 1,243. This figure includes a number of teachers whose salary was paid by the school boards from their surplus funds. The corps of teachers for the entire Island is fixed by the legislature each year when the appropriations to pay their salaries are made, the commissioner being charged with its distribution among the various municipalities, but the school boards may, within certain limitations, increase the number allotted to them provided they pay their salaries from any surplus funds at their disposal. The average number of pupils taught by each teacher was about 63. The average daily attendance was 69,786, or 89.7 per cent, which gives an average of about 58 pupils receiving instruction daily from each teacher. About 59 per cent of the pupils were boys and 41 per cent girls. The average age of all pupils in the rural schools was 10.1 years.

"The above figures show, in a way, the magnitude of the problem to be solved before the people of Porto Rico can assume in full the duties and privileges of self-government. That enormous mass of illiterates, in its primitive, uncured condition, is not safe timber to build the good ship of state. We realize that there are serious social and economic problems to be solved before the people of Porto Rico reach the desired goal. But the pioneer work must be done by the rural school. Those people must be brought to a realization of their condition and to wish to improve it. The rural school, adapted more and more to actual conditions, is the one agency that can bring this about. At present, we are making provision for less than one third of the rural school population. It is as if we had an enormous debt and our resources did not permit us to pay the interest on it. The problem calls for heroic measures.

"Of the 1,243 teachers in charge of the rural schools during the past year, 1,217 or 91 per cent had double enrollment, i.e., one group of 40 pupils or less in the morning for three hours, and another similar group in the afternoon for the same period. The distribution of time among the various subjects of the curriculum depends, of course, on whether the school has double enrollment or not, as well as on the number of grades grouped in any one session.

"The course of study of the rural schools extends over a period of six years. Of the 91,966 different pupils enrolled during the year, 49.1 per cent were found in the first grade, 25.7 per cent in the second, 15.9 per cent in the third, 8.4 per cent in the fourth, and the remaining 0.9 per cent in the fifth and sixth grades. Of the total enrollment 93.2 per cent were on half time, the remaining 6.8 per cent receiving instruction six hours daily.

"Any enrichment of the rural course of study has been necessarily conditioned by the meager professional equipment of the rural teaching force, many of whom entered the service with nothing more than a common-school education and a few scraps of information about school management gotten together for the examination. Up to the present the academic requirements for admission to the examinations for the rural license have been limited to the eighth-grade diploma or its equivalent, and the examinations for the obtention of the license have covered the following subjects: English, Spanish, arithmetic, history of the United States and of Porto Rico, geography, elementary physiology and hygiene, nature study, and methods of teaching. It has been announced already that in all probability candidates for the rural license will have to present four high-school credits for admission to the examinations. The excess of teachers now obtaining and the increasing output of the Normal School will afford opportunity for selection and will raise the standard of efficiency of the force. At its last quarterly meeting the board of trustees of the University of Porto Rico voted to raise the entrance requirements of the Normal Department from four high-school credits to eight. In view of this, the Department of Education will probably increase the requirements for admission to the examinations for the rural license sufficiently to bring them up to the standard established by the board of trustees for admission to the Normal Department of the University.

"The rural teachers are elected by the school boards, subject to the approval of the Commissioner of Education, who pays their salaries from an Insular appropriation. The teachers are divided into three salary classes, as follows: First class, $40; second class, $45; third class, $50. All rural teachers begin at the $40 salary, and after three years of experience pass to the $45 class and after five years to the $50 class. Last year all rural teachers received a salary of $38 only, due to financial embarrassment.

"The rural schools were housed in 1,193 separate buildings, containing a total of 1,250 classrooms. Of these 1,193 rural buildings, 320 are owned by the school boards and were especially constructed for school purposes from plans approved by the Department of Education and the sanitary officials. Most of the rural school buildings contain but one room, although not a few have two, three, and even four, the tendency toward the centralized school growing steadily. In all, 24 new rural school buildings have been erected during the year. Most of these are frame structures, but some are built of reënforced concrete and have a very pleasing appearance."

THE SCHOOL AND THE COMMUNITY

THE movement toward using the schoolhouse as a center for the social activities of the community is gaining ground every year and through this movement the school, as an organization consisting of the teacher and pupils, is rapidly coming to have much more influence in the community life than was formerly the case when the school was considered as merely an organization for the teaching of academic subjects. The need of a social center in the country districts is especially marked, inasmuch as there is a decided tendency among the country people to gather in small groups, based upon relationship or intimate friendship, to the exclusion of the wider interests of the community. Little attempt is usually made to direct in any way the outside activities or the recreation hours of the young people and often their activities take a direction which is distinctly unsocial.

The school in adapting itself to the community in order that it may serve as a social center must make certain investigations, because the need of social service and the kind of service which shall be instituted, depends upon existing local conditions. Some of the most necessary lines of investigation to be made by the teacher and pupils before the most effective aid can be rendered, are those which follow:

First.—The number of farmers who own the farms upon which they live and the number of tenant farmers.

Second.—The average size of the farms; the number of well-arranged homes; the total number of acres devoted to each of the important crops.

Third.—The distance to the nearest market, and the number of miles of well-kept roads.

These three points will determine largely the direction which any social movement must take, because upon them is based the economic situation of the community. In addition to considering the community from the economic point of view, we may also consider the sanitary conditions that prevail in the district, and the teacher and pupils should make a survey of the district with the following points in mind:

First.—The sources of water supply. If water is from open wells, where are they located, and what is the distance from barns and outhouses; are they built in accordance with specifications from the Department of Sanitation?

Second.—How is garbage disposed of in the neighborhood; are common drinking cups and the common towel prohibited in the schoolroom? Is the school furnished with a covered water tank, and does it have facilities for washing the hands and face? Do the people of the neighborhood know the regulations of the Department of Sanitation in regard to sanitary conditions; is there much preventable illness in the district, and to what extent are patent medicines used by the patrons of the school?

Third.—Are the houses, including the schoolhouses, well ventilated and well located as far as distance from standing water or other mosquito-breeding places is concerned? Is the floor of the schoolhouse swept every night, and are foot scrapers and doormats provided? Does the teacher inspect the outhouses, and are they built according to specifications from the Department of Sanitation?

A union of all the patrons of the district is necessary if any movement is to be carried out with telling effect, and the teacher should find out if there is or has been any organization of the men, women, girls, or boys in the district of a social or civic type; has the school done anything up to the present time to improve the social life in the district, and has it ever encouraged local fairs or exhibits of school or agricultural products, and has it founded boys' or girls' agricultural or home economics clubs?

How does the religious condition affect the community, and what is the attitude of the community toward these matters and toward social affairs? How do the young men and young women spend their leisure time? Has the school any magazines or farm papers in its library, and how many homes in the district have any library, or any musical instruments?

What has been the attitude of the previous teachers in the district toward the affairs of the community; how long has each remained in the district? Are changes in the position of the teachers frequent, and if so, what is the reason? Have previous teachers actually resided in the community or have they lived in the nearest town? Have the previous teachers been professionally trained, and have they taken any interest in the affairs of the community outside of their regular school duties?

When the school has succeeded in getting together the information noted in the above paragraphs, it will then be in a position to determine what lines of social activity will be best for the particular community.

The organization of men's clubs and women's clubs for the discussion of topics of general interest and for the purpose of arousing a feeling of community interest should be undertaken as soon as possible, the teacher always remembering that the management of these organizations should be in the hands of the members who compose them, and that the teacher should act only as an adviser in case advice may be necessary. The people should feel that on them rests the responsibility of developing the civic and social life of the community, and the teacher should not allow them to shift this responsibility. The organization of boys' clubs and girls' clubs will present no difficulties to the teacher who has made a study of the situation and who is prepared for his work. The boys and girls are in the most easily influenced period of their lives, and whether or not they will develop a sense of civic and social responsibility, depends very largely upon the attitude which their teachers take in regard to these matters.

Rural life in any community has a tendency to be monotonous and deadening to the finer qualities. Uninterrupted and unduly prolonged physical labor tends to the detriment of both the physical and the mental abilities of the individual. The isolation of the country home tends to narrow and restrict social intercourse, and the difficulty of travel and communication increases the monotony of country life. These circumstances do a great deal to offset the advantage of living in the country and have contributed a great deal to the stigma that has always been attached to the countryman.

If there is to be any reform in this isolated social life of the community, the reform must come about through the schools. The Government can aid to a great extent through the provision of well-kept roads and by the establishment of means of communication such as the telephone and the telegraph. The man who is in touch with the large affairs of life forgets his own petty annoyances in the contemplation of problems of greater importance, while the man who has nothing to think about except the annoyances of his own life tends to become self-centered and narrow.

Rural social center work in the United States has made great progress within the last few years and has been successful in practically all the places where it has been tried, especially if the teacher is a person of tact and intelligence. A great deal depends upon the attitude which the teacher has in this work, and it is not enough that the teacher should undertake such work as a burden added to the already overcrowded curriculum of the day, but the teacher should enter into the movement with a sincere desire to improve the condition of the community and bring the patrons of the district to a higher degree of efficiency as workmen and as citizens. In every community there are many young women and young men who are above the average school age who are compelled to work during the day, and who are fast becoming fixed in the monotonous life that has surrounded the older people of the community, who might easily be interested by the teacher and influenced through the formation of social clubs, so that they would form the nucleus for a better coming generation of citizens. The meetings of young people should partake of recreation as well as of serious study, and while the avowed intention of new clubs formed by the school should be for the purpose of bettering the social and civic condition of the people of the community, they must be placed in as favorable a light as possible, for it should be remembered that people will often undertake a movement which will have decidedly beneficial results if it is disguised under the form of recreation, when they would hesitate to give their continued assistance to such a movement if it partook entirely of the nature of serious study.

The Department of Education in the Island of Porto Rico is making a special effort at the present time to interest the older girls and the women of the towns in social betterment through the medium of mothers' clubs and girls' clubs, organized under the direction of the teachers of home economics. These clubs have been organized in practically all of the towns of the Island and are meeting with general success. In many cases the girls' clubs assume an aspect of economic improvement in that they undertake the production of certain salable articles such as embroidery or handwork, and the teacher in charge of the group provides the market for the articles produced. Little has been done up to the present in organizing the men and boys into social groups. Boy scout organizations were widely established through the Island several years ago, but on account of the lack of some individual to devote his time to the organizing side of the movement they have decreased in number and in influence. Anyone who is at all familiar with the social situation in Porto Rico, especially in the rural districts, will see at once the necessity of organizations of the kind mentioned above and will be impressed with the possibilities for good in a community which can be exercised by the rural school under the direction of an efficient, well trained, enthusiastic teacher. The democratic form of government which the Island enjoys demands the highest possible development of civic and social ideas and obligations, and in order to fulfill its highest mission the school should undertake such lines of work as will tend to develop not only better educated people of academic attainments, but also better trained citizens in the social and civic sense.

RELATION OF THE TEACHER TO THE COMMUNITY

IN rural sections the school should be a factor of much more importance than it is in the urban centers for the reason that the country people are almost entirely shut off from other educative institutions such as public libraries, free lectures, and association with their fellow-citizens, privileges which the urban resident is able to use to great advantage. To carry out effectively the mission of the rural school in a community and to make it a center from which there may be spread an influence for social betterment, as well as for intellectual improvement, the teacher is the all-important factor. There are certain duties which a teacher owes to his profession, in case he is working in the country, which cannot be neglected if he is to obtain the results which he should obtain. Following are some of the most important of these duties:

First.—The teacher should visit all homes and get acquainted with the patrons. This is important in order that he may get an insight into the conditions under which the people are living, and that he may know the particular difficulties of the pupils with whom he has to deal. Moreover, acquaintance on the part of the parents with the teacher will often aid in avoiding disciplinary difficulties, inasmuch as the parents come to have increasing confidence in him and his work as their acquaintance with him increases.

Second.—The teacher should study conditions from all angles so as to adapt the school work to the needs of the community. Even in so small an island as Porto Rico, we have distinctly different occupations centered in different parts of the Island, and the teacher should remember that the majority of his pupils will undoubtedly grow up to take a part in the prevailing industry of the community in which they are born and raised. The schedule and work of the rural school should not be an attempt to imitate the plan of study of the urban schools, inasmuch as the problems are entirely different, and until a teacher has convinced himself of this fact and has made an attempt to model his work on the needs of the community, the school will not accomplish its full mission.

Third.—The teacher should live in the district seven days in the week during the school term. More and more the idea is becoming prevalent that rural teachers should be provided with a house and a small plot of ground near the school in order to become permanent residents of the district. The average farmer is very conservative and needs visual demonstration of the merits of new ideas before he will accept them. No amount of theoretical teaching will improve farming conditions to any great extent, and unless the teacher is able to become a demonstrator of his ideas by actually putting them into practice on the plot of ground which he himself manages, he cannot expect to influence to any great extent the agricultural movements of the community in which he works. The school should aim not only for the education of the children who are actually enrolled, but also for the betterment of the agricultural and social conditions of the community.

Fourth.—The rural teacher should be loyal to his pupils and patrons. The teacher who feels himself an individual superior to the members of the community whom he is serving and allows this feeling to express itself in his attitude toward them, loses the greater part of his influence through this action. The countryman likes to be met on equal terms and does not enjoy a condescending attitude any more than does his brother who lives in the town. The teacher should have in mind only the benefits which he may bring to the community, and if he actually and actively takes part in the social movements of the place he will come to learn that human nature is the same in the country as in the town, and he will be able to acquire a sincere liking for the people with whom he works.

Fifth.—The teacher should so conduct himself outside of the school as to win respect for himself and for his profession. The idea that a teacher's duty to the school ends with the closing of the actual school day is a mistaken one. Any action on the part of the teacher outside of his school work which would tend to lower him in the estimation of his pupils or their parents, inevitably tends to reduce the amount of influence which he can exert. A teacher is on duty constantly and cannot limit his working hours or his working habits to certain defined periods of time.

Sixth.—The teacher should stay more than one year in a district, unless a change means decided professional and financial advancement. Short term teachers are often of more harm than benefit to the children of a community. The advent of a new teacher means a change in plans and usually a change in methods of work. These changes tend to upset the minds of the children who naturally like to follow well-defined lines of work. The constant change of teachers also means that none of them stays sufficiently long to learn the needs of the community and the best method of meeting these needs. School boards should offer inducements to rural teachers in the way of increasing the salary for increased length of service, and thus there would be less desire on the part of the teacher to move from one district to another.

Seventh.—The teacher should arouse an interest in the school and do his part to convince the patrons of the need of a better school to meet the demands of the present day. A great part of the teacher's work lies outside of his actual teaching, and more and more we are coming to conceive the school as a social as well as an educational institution, and by means of parents' meetings, using the school as a social center and making the schoolhouse a gathering place for the patrons of the district, where they may meet and discuss the problems with which they are confronted, the present-day teacher supplements his actual teaching duties. There are few other ways in which the social needs of the country people can be better met than through the rural school. Moreover, by means of these meetings it is possible to show parents the progress which is being made by their children in the school work and to impress them with the necessity of regular and punctual attendance. One of the surest ways to win the approval of men and women is by interesting them in the progress of their children, and the wise teacher will take advantage of every opportunity which presents itself, and go to great lengths to make opportunities for cultivating the interest of the parents in the school, through this means.

Eighth.—The teacher in a rural school should have as the aim of rural education "better men, better farming, and better living." The country teacher who appreciates and realizes this is aware of the chief factors in the solution of the farm problem. He must also remember that he is a public servant and that the public has a right to expect him to put his whole soul into the welfare of the community. The schools are held to be largely responsible for ineffective farming and the low ideals of country life. A great many of our rural teachers are not at all in sympathy with rural ideals and rural customs. They regard their position as merely temporary, and express, even though it may be involuntary on their part, the idea that the town is much preferable to the country, and in this way inculcate in the children a distaste for the life of the country, when it should be their duty to present the best features of rural life in order to persuade the children to remain on the farms.

Ninth.—The teacher should be able to discriminate between essentials and non-essentials and omit the latter, thus giving more time to the problems of country life. He should get away from the formalism of textbooks, using them only as tools, and adapt all his work to the needs and interests of the community. He should not attempt to be too scientific, but should teach in terms of child life. And even in his intercourse with the patrons of the school he should put himself, in manners and conversation, on terms of equality with them. The teacher should learn to use his energy for better and more definite planning, and in the schoolroom should do for the children fewer of those things that may be done by the pupils themselves. There is no reason why pupils should not be taught to study and work independently, and the school that fulfills its highest mission trains children to become independent workers. Especially is this true in the country, where pupils should work as well as study and recite. Mere academic training in the rural school will defeat the purpose of the school and will be very apt to produce young men and young women who are dissatisfied with the conditions under which they must live after leaving school.

PRESENT-DAY RURAL SCHOOL MOVEMENTS

WITHIN the last few years, rural education in the United States has received a great deal of attention, and many plans have been suggested for the betterment of rural teaching. Conferences of state and national educators have been held for the purpose of discussing the rural school question, and out of the mass of school movements, discussions, and ideas which have been presented, there are some which might be made applicable to the situation as it exists in Porto Rico.

The following ideas seem to indicate the spirit which underlies rural education of the present day. They are the result of a conference held in Kentucky in 1914 by people who were especially interested in rural school problems:

First.—The greatest social need of the century is the organization and consequent up-building of the rural life of America.

Second.—This must be the outgrowth of the self-activity of rural life forces.

Third.—Outside forces can only assist in the work.

Fourth.—There is a need of raising the general level of living in the country in order to keep the brightest and best people from leaving the country in too great numbers.

Fifth.—To educate the young in the schools, to elevate their ideals, to arouse their ambitions without raising the level of living and offering them a broader field for the exercise of their talents, may do as much harm as good.

Sixth.—The school is only one of the agencies for community up-building.

Seventh.—There must be coöperation among the rural life forces, all working together for a common end.

Eighth.—The farmer, the country woman, the country teacher, the country editor, the country doctor, and the country business man must all join hands for better living along every line in the country.

Ninth.—The community is the proper unit for rural development.

Tenth.—The community must learn how to educate, to organize, and to develop itself.

In attempting to carry out the ideas expressed in the statements quoted above, emphasis has been laid upon educational rallies, school farms, farmers' Chatauquas, and other means which have as their aim the idea of arousing community pride and community coöperation, not only for the benefit and betterment of the school, but also for the benefit and betterment of the members of the community who are not of school age. A great deal of emphasis has been laid upon rural school extension work, that is, work carried on under the supervision of school officers but which really devotes its main efforts to adults who are living in rural communities. One of the most recent steps in this direction was the passing of the bill known as the "Smith Lever Act" by the Federal Congress in 1914, which ultimately carries with it an appropriation of over $4,500,000 for agricultural extension and rural welfare. Under this bill, Porto Rico receives $10,000 per year for extension work among the farmers, the work being carried out under the supervision of the Federal Experiment Station located at Mayaguez.

Another movement which is prominent in rural school affairs at present, is the tendency toward a larger unit of organization for taxation and administration. The rural schools of Porto Rico are already under the municipal unit of school administration, which probably will not be changed, as close supervision demands rather small units of organization. In the report of the Commissioner of Education for 1915-16 a suggestion is made that the appropriation of money for schools throughout the Island be determined by the school population in a given community and not by the taxable wealth of that community. It frequently happens that the wealthiest municipalities are the ones which are least in need of additional school facilities, and this recommendation tends to make the unit for school taxation and appropriation of funds an Insular rather than a municipal unit, as we have to-day. The idea, of course, is based upon the fact that Porto Rico is small enough so that every citizen should be interested in the education of all the children of the Island, and that the movements in education should be Insular in unit rather than municipal.

Demonstration schools for rural communities have been organized with a view to showing the people in a definite and concrete way what a school can do for a community. These demonstration schools are usually placed in a central location and put under the charge of the teachers of greatest experience and ability. All of the children in the different grades included in the rural school course have a course of study to complete in the schoolroom, and another equally emphasized course of study to complete in the home and on the farm.

Experiments and studies are being carried on which involve the use of every day throughout the year. To accomplish this end, the father and mother have become the assistant supervisors of the home work and the farm work, and they receive the advice, the suggestion, and the instruction of the rural supervisors of schools. While working to get the best possible results from the efforts made, and to establish the facts by samples, by photographs, and by financial relations of cost and return, these undertakings are accompanied by neighborhood meetings of many kinds which have had the effect of enlarging community interest, community support, and community improvement. Out of these efforts have come better social conditions, more harmonious relations, a development of better ideals, and a higher conception of life.

These demonstration schools, in addition to being a force among the people in the community where they are located, also serve as educational centers which are to be visited by the other rural teachers of the community in order that the inexperienced and untrained teacher may receive the benefit of the teacher of more experience. In addition, these schools also serve the purpose of experimental schools where many ideas are worked out and put into effect, and new methods of teaching as well as untried methods of farming are given a trial.

The rural school situation is being studied more to-day than ever before, for it is being realized that our country schools are not functioning to the best advantage. The social side of the task, extension work among the patrons of the district, consolidated and more efficient schools, and better trained teachers are only a few of the phases of this movement toward making the rural school a real force throughout the country. The movement is gaining ground each year, and though there are many problems to be solved and many difficult situations to be met, yet there is every reason to believe that out of this mass of experiments there will evolve the rural school of the future, which will be a more vital factor in the community than has been the case up to the present day.

PHYSICAL DEVELOPMENT AND LONGEVITY

THE anthropometric examinations given in the University of Porto Rico during the last two years have provided data from which to determine the physical development of the Porto Rican. A total of 1,412 examinations has been made, including 616 men and 796 women. These students ranged in age from fifteen to thirty years.

A comparison of the physical development of American and Porto Rican boys and girls of the same age shows that the Porto Rican surpasses the American in nearly every point, at the ages of fifteen, sixteen, and seventeen. At eighteen the physical development is about the same, but from that time there seems to be little additional growth on the part of the Porto Rican, while the American continues to develop up to and including the twenty-second year. This seems to confirm the generally accepted theory that a person matures earlier in the tropics than he does in a temperate climate. That the slighter physical development is the effect of geographic or climatic conditions, and is not entirely due to race, is proved by the fact that measurements of Chilean boys, who are of Spanish blood, more nearly approximate those of North American boys than they do those of Porto Ricans. The following tables show a comparison of the development of the Porto Rican students with the average development of American men and women. The measurements are in pounds and inches.

Table I

	Average measurements of Porto Rican male students from 16 to 28 years of age	Average measurements of American men from 17 to 30 years of age
Height	64.94	67.6
Weight	110.67	138.6
Chest, transversal	10.26	10.8
Chest, anterior-posterior	7.92	7.5
Shoulders	15.06	16.1

Neck	13.05	13.9
Chest, contracted	30.63	33.7
Chest, expanded	33.25	36.7
Waist	27.92	29.1
Right forearm	9.33	10.4
Left forearm	9.20	10.4
Right arm up	9.61	11.9
Right arm down	8.45	10.4
Left arm up	9.42	11.8
Left arm down	8.22	10.3
Right thigh	17.97	20.3
Left thigh	17.83	20.2
Right calf	12.64	13.8
Left calf	12.66	13.8

Table II

	Average measurements of Porto Rican women students from 16 to 28 years of age	Average measurements of American women from 17 to 30 years of age
Height	61.78	62.9
Weight	107.82	116.0

Chest, transversal	9.35	10.0
Chest, anterior-posterior	6.93	6.8
Shoulders	13.64	14.4
Neck	11.98	12.1
Chest, natural	29.19	29.7
Chest, contracted	28.57	29.6
Chest, expanded	31.29	32.0
Waist	25.14	24.3
Hips	33.76	35.7
Right forearm	8.71	8.8
Left forearm	8.61	8.6
Right arm down	8.44	9.8
Left arm down	8.40	9.7
Right arm up	8.99	10.8
Left arm up	8.82	10.6
Right thigh	18.79	21.1
Left thigh	18.65	21.0
Right calf	12.66	13.0
Left calf	12.64	13.0

If it is true that the Porto Rican reaches the height of physical development at the age of eighteen, then we may consider that an average of the measurements of the men and women from and after that age will give us what is practically the representative physical development of the Porto Rican adult. These averages are found in the following table.

TABLE III

Representative development of Porto Rican students at the University of Porto Rico, of more than 18 years of age.

	Men	Women
Height	65.87	61.83
Weight	116.21	107.93
Shoulders	15.39	13.67
Chest, transversal	10.39	9.34
Chest, anterior-posterior	8.07	6.98
Neck	13.32	12.01
Chest, muscular	32.74	30.27
Chest, natural	31.87	29.45
Chest, expanded	33.84	31.30
Chest, contracted	31.36	28.23
Waist	27.96	25.08
Hips	32.13	33.45
Right arm down	8.62	8.49
Right arm up	9.79	8.95
Right forearm	9.53	8.61

Left arm down	8.43	8.36
Left arm up	9.61	8.83
Left forearm	9.46	8.29
Right thigh	18.38	18.76
Left thigh	18.15	18.61
Right calf	12.85	12.68
Left calf	12.90	12.64

For the purpose of comparing the Porto Rican boys with boys of Spanish blood, but of another climate, Table IV, which shows the comparative development of Porto Rican and Chilean boys from 16 to 20 years of age, is given. The measurements for the Chilean boys were furnished by the Museo Nacional of Santiago, Chili.

Table IV

Sixteen years	Porto Rico	Chili
Number observed	16.00	340.00
Height	64.42	64.49
Weight	105.44	123.64
Chest	31.01	33.09
Chest, transversal	9.69	10.34
Chest, anterior-posterior	7.79	7.66
Waist	27.28	25.11
Seventeen years		
Number observed	75.00	248.00

Height	64.41	65.43
Weight	113.41	128.48
Chest	32.06	33.52
Chest, transversal	10.11	10.72
Chest, anterior-posterior	7.99	7.97
Waist	25.05	25.54

Eighteen years

Number observed	92.00	138.00
Height	65.72	65.86
Weight	118.43	133.32
Chest	32.61	34.33
Chest, transversal	10.36	11.04
Chest, anterior-posterior	8.14	8.09
Waist	28.08	26.09

Nineteen years

Number observed	107.00	65.00
Height	65.47	65.94
Weight	111.53	133.98
Chest	32.33	34.66
Chest, transversal	10.27	11.35
Chest, anterior-posterior	8.15	8.17
Waist	27.15	26.13

Twenty years

Number observed	78.00	18.00
Height	65.91	66.18
Weight	113.32	113.52
Chest	32.36	34.71
Chest, transversal	10.39	11.43
Chest, anterior-posterior	7.77	8.33
Waist	27.58	26.44

A study of the census of 1910 showing the distribution of the population of Porto Rico by race and by age periods gives some interesting information. If the situation given there is taken to be typical of general conditions, by considering the number of children of each class under one year of age, we find that the highest birth rate is among the mulattoes; next in order come the native whites of native parentage, next the blacks, and last the native whites of foreign or mixed parentage. The actual percentage of each class under one year of age is as follows: mulattoes, 3.9 per cent; native whites of native parentage, 3.6 per cent; blacks, 2.5 per cent; native whites of foreign or mixed parentage, 2 per cent. The percentage of the population under five years of age in each class tends to confirm this statement. It is as follows: mulattoes 17.9 per cent; native whites of native parentage, 14.7 per cent; blacks, 12.2 per cent; native whites of foreign or mixed parentage, 9.5 per cent.

While the mulattoes have the highest birth rate, it is also true that, as a general thing, they are the shortest lived of any of the classes mentioned. The class which generally has greatest longevity consists of the negroes; next in order come the native whites of mixed or foreign parentage, then the native whites of native parentage, and last, the mulattoes. Thus the order, as regards length of life, is nearly the reverse of what it is as regards birth rate.

It is observed also that while native whites of foreign or mixed parentage have a comparatively great length of life and a comparatively low birth rate, their children, who fall in the class of native whites of native parentage, have shorter lives and tend to produce larger families, than did the parents. In each class the females outnumber the males, the proportion being 100 females to 99.4 males for the total population, which, however, includes the foreign-born whites, where the males outnumber the females. In the classes of native-born citizens, the difference between the numbers of the sexes is greater than the ratio for the total population would indicate, being the greatest among the mulattoes, where the ratio is 93.6 males for every 100 females. In each class it is found that the women enjoy greater length of life than do the men.

The following table shows what proportion of the total number of each class of the population falls under the age groups designated.

Table V

	Negroes		Mulattoes		Native White of native parentage		Native White of foreign or mixed parentage		Foreign born white	
	Males	Females	Males	Females	Males	Females	Males	Females	Males	Females
Under 5 years	12.9	11.6	18.3	17.4	17.1	16.4	10.1	8.9	.8	2.1
5 to 24 years	42.3	42.5	48.2	47.1	46.2	46.4	45.6	45.9	18.8	20.8
25 to 54 years	34.4	34.8	29.0	30.1	31.7	31.5	36.6	35.6	64.6	57.2
55 to 84 years	9.7	10.5	4.4	5.3	5.0	5.0	7.4	9.3	15.6	19.2
85 years and over	.7	.8	.1	.2	.1	.2	.1	.3	.2	.8

It will be noticed that above the age of 55 there is a larger proportion of women than men in each class. Judging the median age for each group to be the year which divides the total number of that group into two equal divisions, so far as number is concerned, we find the following median ages: blacks, 23; mulattoes, 18; native whites of native parentage, 20; native whites of foreign or mixed parentage, 22; foreign-born whites, 37. These results correspond exactly with the statements previously made regarding the longevity of each group. This would, of course, only give the median age for each class at the time the census was taken, in 1910, but as practically the same age distribution is also found in the census of 1899, it may be concluded that the results are approximately correct. This means that 50 per cent of each group does not live beyond the age indicated, and is sometimes known as the "mean length of life." Data for calculating the average length of life are not available.

A comparison of the age groups in the United States and in Porto Rico shows that the proportion in the younger ages is greater in Porto Rico than it is in the United States.

Table VI

	Native white		Colored	
	Porto Rico	United States	Porto Rico	United States
Under 5 years	16.5	13.5	17.1	12.9
5 to 14 years	26.3	23.0	27.1	24.4
15 to 24 years	20.0	20.3	19.8	21.3
25 to 44 years	25.4	26.5	24.2	26.8
45 to 64 years	9.6	13.0	9.4	11.3
65 years and over	2.2	3.6	2.4	3.0

Undoubtedly the work of the Department of Sanitation and of the Institute of Tropical Medicine will do much to change the death rate within the next few years, and to prolong life. We may well expect the next census to show a much larger percentage of the population in the higher age groups.

FOOTNOTES:

[1] The difference in numbers between men and women living together consensually is doubtless due to the fact that many men who have legitimate wives also have consensual wives or mistresses.

[2] This would indicate that many of the divorced men had remarried and were listed in the census as married instead of divorced.

Milton Keynes UK
Ingram Content Group UK Ltd.
UKHW011124180424
441376UK00004B/199